New Thresholds of Faith

By Kenneth E. Hagin

Unless otherwise indicated, all Scripture quotations in this volume are from the *King James Version* of the Bible.

Second Edition
Eighth Printing 1992

ISBN 0-89276-070-2

In the U.S. write:
Kenneth Hagin Ministries
P.O. Box 50126
Tulsa, OK 74150-0126

In Canada write:
Kenneth Hagin Ministries
P.O. Box 335
Islington (Toronto), Ontario
Canada, M9A 4X3

BOOKS BY KENNETH E. HAGIN

* *New Thresholds of Faith*
* *Prevailing Prayer to Peace*
* *Concerning Spiritual Gifts*
  Bible Faith Study Course
  Bible Prayer Study Course
  The Holy Spirit and His Gifts
* *The Ministry Gifts (Study Guide)*
  Seven Things You Should Know About Divine Healing
  El Shaddai
  Zoe: The God-Kind of Life
  A Commonsense Guide to Fasting
  Must Christians Suffer?
  The Woman Question
  The Believer's Authority
  Ministering to Your Family
  What To Do When Faith Seems Weak and Victory Lost
  Growing Up, Spiritually
  Bodily Healing and the Atonement
  Exceedingly Growing Faith
  Understanding the Anointing
  I Believe in Visions
  Understanding How To Fight the Good Fight of Faith
  Plans, Purposes, and Pursuits
  How You Can Be Led by the Spirit of God
  A Fresh Anointing
  Your Faith in God Will Work
  The Art of Prayer

BOOKS BY KENNETH HAGIN JR.
* *Man's Impossibility — God's Possibility*
  Because of Jesus
  The Key to the Supernatural
* *Faith Worketh by Love*
  Blueprint for Building Strong Faith
* *Seven Hindrances to Healing*
* *The Past Tense of God's Word*
  How To Make the Dream God Gave You Come True
  Faith Takes Back What the Devil's Stolen
  "The Prison Door Is Open — What Are You Still Doing Inside?"
  Itching Ears
  Where Do We Go From Here?
  How To Be a Success in Life
  Get Acquainted With God
  Showdown With the Devil
  Unforgiveness
  The Answer for Oppression
  Is Your Miracle Passing You By?
  Commanding Power
  The Life of Obedience
  Ministering to the Brokenhearted
  God's Irresistible Word
  Healing: Forever Settled
  Don't Quit! Your Faith Will See You Through
  The Untapped Power in Praise

*These titles are also available in Spanish. Information about other foreign translations of several of the above titles (i.e., Finnish, French, German, Indonesian, Polish, Russian, etc.) may be obtained by writing to: Kenneth Hagin Ministries, P.O. Box 50126, Tulsa, Oklahoma 74150-0126.

Contents

Lesson 1

How Do We Get Faith?

Bible Texts: Romans 10:8-10,13,14,17; Acts 11:13,14; 14:7-10; 8:5-8

Central Truth: God has provided the way whereby everyone can have faith.

We read in Hebrews 11:6, *"But without faith it is impossible to please him: for he that cometh to God must believe that he is, and that he is a rewarder of them that diligently seek him."*

If God demands we have faith when it is impossible for us to have faith, we have a right to challenge His justice. But if He places within our hands the means whereby faith can be produced, then the responsibility rests with us whether or not we have faith.

God has told us without faith it is impossible to please Him. But He also has told us how to get faith. If we don't have faith, it is not God's fault. To blame God for our lack of faith is nothing but ignorance. God has provided the way whereby everyone can have faith.

Faith for Salvation

The Apostle Paul said we are saved by faith. *"For by grace are ye saved through faith; and that not of yourselves: it is the gift of God"* (Eph. 2:8). But how do you get faith to be saved?

ROMANS 10:8-10,13,14,17

8 But what saith it? The word is nigh thee, even in thy mouth, and in thy heart: that is, the word of faith, which we preach;

9 That if thou shalt confess with thy mouth the Lord Jesus, and shalt believe in thine heart that God hath raised him from the dead, thou shalt be saved.

10 For with the heart man believeth unto righteousness; and with the mouth confession is made unto salvation. . . .

13 For whosoever shall call upon the name of the Lord shall be saved.

14 How then shall they call on him in whom they have not believed? and how shall they believe in him of whom they have not heard? and how shall they hear without a preacher? . . .

17 So then faith cometh by hearing, and hearing by the word of God.

After studying the passage of Scripture quoted above, what three steps does man take to receive salvation? (1. Confess 2. Believe 3. Accept.) To whom is this salvation available, according to verse 13? (Whosoever.) According to verse 17, where does faith come from? (By hearing the Word of God.)

ACTS 11:13,14

13 And he shewed us how he [Cornelius] had seen an angel in his house, which stood and said unto him, Send men to Joppa, and call for Simon, whose surname is Peter;

14 Who shall tell thee words, whereby thou and all thy house shall be saved.

God instructed Cornelius to send for Peter in order to learn the plan of

1

salvation. In the Great Commission, recorded in Mark 16:15-18, Jesus told His disciples, *"Go ye into all the world, and preach the gospel to every creature ..."* Cornelius had not yet heard this glorious Gospel. He was not saved. God told Cornelius to send for Peter in order to learn the plan of salvation.

Why did Cornelius have to send for Peter? Why couldn't the angel have explained the plan of salvation to Cornelius just as well? (Angels cannot preach the Gospel. God has given this task to man.)

The verse *"Who shall tell thee words, whereby thou and all thy house shall be saved"* shows us that men are saved by hearing words! The reason for this is because *"faith cometh by hearing, and hearing by the word of God"* (Rom. 10:17).

Faith for Healing

ACTS 14:7-10

7 And there they [Paul and Barnabas] preached the gospel.
8 And there sat a certain man at Lystra, impotent in his feet, being a cripple from his mother's womb, who never had walked:
9 The same heard Paul speak: who stedfastly beholding him, and perceiving that he had faith to be healed,
10 Said with a loud voice, Stand upright on thy feet. And he leaped and walked.

A casual reader of the Word once said concerning this passage of Scripture, "Isn't it wonderful how Paul healed that man?" However, Paul did not heal the man. The man was not healed because Paul was an apostle.

He was not healed through Paul's faith. The man himself had the faith.

Paul did three things:
1. He preached the Gospel (v. 7).
2. He perceived that the man had faith to be healed (v. 9).
3. He told the man to stand up and walk (v. 10).

The man did three things:
1. He heard Paul preach (v. 9).
2. He had faith to be healed (v. 9).
3. He leaped and walked (v. 10).

The man was not healed by some power Paul had. The man himself had faith to be healed.

Where did the man get the faith to be healed? **By hearing Paul speak.** What did Paul speak? **He preached the Gospel.** Paul preached a Gospel of salvation and healing: *"For I am not ashamed of the gospel of Christ: for it is the power of God unto salvation to every one that believeth; to the Jew first, and also to the Greek"* (Rom. 1:16).

A footnote in the Scofield Bible referring to this verse says, "The Greek and Hebrew words for salvation imply the ideas of deliverance, safety, preservation, healing, and soundness." Therefore, Paul was saying, "I am not ashamed of the Gospel of Christ. It is the power of God unto deliverance, safety, preservation, healing, and soundness." Paul preached the *full* Gospel; not just part of it.

ACTS 8:5-8

5 Then Philip went down to the city of Samaria, and preached Christ unto them.
6 And the people with one accord gave heed unto those things which Philip spake,

2

hearing and seeing the miracles which he did.

7 For unclean spirits, crying with loud voice, came out of many that were possessed with them: and many taken with palsies, and that were lame, were healed.

8 And there was great joy in that city.

The great miracles recorded in the above verses came about as the result of Philip's preaching Christ. The New Testament knows no Christ without Christ the Healer. Physical healing is part of the Gospel. If there is no Gospel of healing today, then neither is there a Gospel of salvation.

Faith in Action

P. C. Nelson, who was for many years a noted Baptist minister, said, "Healing is part and parcel of the Gospel." While pastoring a church in Detroit, Michigan, in 1921, he was struck by an automobile. The doctors said his left leg probably would have to be amputated. Even if they didn't have to take it off, it would be stiff.

As he lay in bed, the verses of Scripture in James 5:14,15 came to him: *"Is any sick among you? let him call for the elders of the church; and let them pray over him, anointing him with oil in the name of the Lord: And the prayer of faith shall save the sick, and the Lord shall raise him up; and if he have committed sins, they shall be forgiven him."*

Dr. Nelson tried to excuse himself to the Lord by saying that they didn't practice this in his church. The Lord reminded him that he had four Spirit-filled friends who believed in it, and He told Dr. Nelson to call them to come and pray for him. They came to his home, anointed him with oil, and prayed the prayer of faith for him. He was healed. His leg didn't have to be removed, and it was never stiff. *"Faith cometh by hearing, and hearing by the word of God."*

Many years ago, as a young Baptist boy, I lay on the bed of sickness. As I read Grandma Drake's "Methodist" Bible, I realized that I had never heard the *full* Gospel, just part of it. The more I read, the more I saw that I didn't have to die. The more I studied the Bible, the more I realized I could be healed!

The devil was right there, of course, bringing to my remembrance all the doubt and unbelief I had ever heard. He told me that healing had been done away with. (Fortunately, I couldn't remember ever hearing that faith had been done away with.) I also had to struggle with the teaching that God would heal *if* He wanted to. (This, however, was an even bigger insult to God than saying that He couldn't.)

I read in Mark 5:34 where Jesus spoke to the woman with the issue of blood, saying, *"Daughter, thy faith hath made thee whole; go in peace, and be whole of thy plague."* Jesus didn't say His power had made her whole; He said, *"Daughter THY FAITH hath made thee whole..."* When I saw this, I knew then that if *her* faith had made her whole, *my* faith could make me whole. And, thank God, it did.

My paralysis disappeared, my

heart condition became normal, and I've been going at a hop, skip, and jump ever since, preaching the Gospel in its fullness for more than 50 years.

Memory Text:
"So then faith cometh by hearing, and hearing by the word of God" (Rom. 10:17).

THE LESSON IN ACTION: *"But be ye doers of the word, and not hearers only..."* (James 1:22).

What Is Faith?

Bible Texts: Hebrews 11:1; Mark 11:23,24; John 20:24-29;
Romans 4:17-21

Central Truth: Faith is grasping the unrealities of hope and bringing
them into the realm of reality.

A key verse in the study of faith is the familiar one found in Hebrews 11:1, *"Now faith is the substance of things hoped for, the evidence of things not seen."* Moffatt's translation of this verse reads, "Now faith means that we are confident of what we hope for, convinced of what we do not see."

Another translation says, "Faith is giving substance to things hoped for." Still another translation reads, "Faith is the warranty deed, the thing for which we have finally hoped is at last ours." Here God is telling us what faith is.

There are a number of kinds of faith. Everyone, saved and unsaved alike, has a natural, human faith. The above Scripture, however, is talking about a supernatural faith — a faith that believes with the heart rather than believing what our physical senses may tell us. Faith, in other words, is grasping the unrealities of hope and bringing them into the realm of reality. And faith grows out of the Word of God.

Our text describes faith as *"the evidence of things not seen."* For example, you hope for finances to meet the obligations you have to pay. Faith gives the assurance that you will have

the money when you need it. You hope for physical strength to do the work that you must do. Faith says, *"The Lord is the strength of my life; of whom shall I be afraid?"* (Ps. 27:1). Faith will say about itself everything that the Word says, for *faith in God is simply faith in His Word.*

I learned an important lesson in faith shortly after I was raised up from the bed of sickness many years ago. I needed work, and since this was during the Depression, work was not easy to find. I was able to get a job in a nursery helping pull up peach trees. With another boy on the other side of the tree, together we would pull up these two-year-old trees to fill orders that had come in. This was really hard work — especially since I had been bedfast for 16 months and at this time had been up only a few months.

Each day the number of workers would be fewer and fewer, and each day someone would say to me. "Well, I didn't think you'd make it today. You know, two or three quit yesterday."

"If it weren't for the Lord I wouldn't be here," I would answer. "You see, His strength is my strength. The Bible says, *'The Lord is the strength of my life . . .'* My life consists of the physical as well as the spiritual, and the Lord is the strength of my life."

If I had gone according to my feelings, I wouldn't have gotten out of bed. I acted on the Word because I knew what faith was. I never received any strength until I started to work.

Many people want to receive and then believe they've got it. It doesn't work that way, though. You have to believe first, and then you will receive.

So I would pull myself out of bed each morning and go to work, gaining strength as I went along, trusting in God's Word. Although I was the weakest and skinniest one among that group of men, I was the last one to stay on the job.

We may say we know God's Word is good, but we will never really know until we have acted on it and have reaped its results. Faith is giving substance to things hoped for.

I went to work. I acted on God's Word. I hoped for physical strength to do the work I knew must be done, and as I acted on God's Word, my faith gave substance to that which I hoped for. Hope says, "I'll have it *sometime.*" Faith says, "I have it *now.*"

Head Faith vs. Heart Faith

John Wesley once said that the devil has given the Church a substitute for faith; one that looks and sounds so much like faith that few people can tell the difference. This sub-stitute he called "mental assent." Many people read God's Word and agree that it is true, but they are agreeing only with their minds. And that is not what gets the job done. It is heart faith that receives from God.

MARK 11:23,24
23 For verily I say unto you, That whosoever shall say unto this mountain, Be thou removed, and be thou cast into the sea; and shall not doubt in his heart, but shall believe that those things which he saith shall come to pass; he shall have whatsoever he saith.
24 Therefore I say unto you, What things soever ye desire, when ye pray, believe that ye receive them, and ye shall have them.

How can we tell whether we have this heart faith or we are just mentally agreeing? Mental assent says, "I know God's Word is true. I know God has promised healing, but for some reason I can't get it; I can't understand it." However, real faith in God's Word says, "If God's Word says it's so, then it's so. It is mine. I have it now. I have it even though I can't see it."

I've heard people say, "But the thing I have been praying about hasn't come to pass yet." If you already had it, you wouldn't have to believe it, for then you would know it. You have to take that step of *believing* in order to come to the place of *knowing.* Too many people want to know it from the standpoint of its coming to pass, and then believe it. We must believe it because God's Word *says* it is ours. *Then* it materializes.

Notice from Mark 11:24 that the receiving comes *after* the believing:

"What things soever ye desire, when ye pray, believe that ye receive them, and ye shall have them." Jesus was simply saying, "You've got to believe you have it before you can receive it."

I never have been able to receive physical healing for myself without first *believing* I have it. Every symptom in my body cries out, "You don't have it." I simply stand firm on what God's Word says about my healing and continue to claim that I am healed. Results are then forthcoming. But if I were to sit around, groan and sigh, gripe, and complain, waiting until every symptom was gone and my feelings corresponded with my faith before I believed, I never would get very far, because *"faith is ... the evidence of things not seen."*

Thomas' Faith vs. Abraham's Faith

Too many Christians have a "Thomas faith" when they should have an "Abraham faith." Thomas said, "I'll not believe until I can see Him," whereas "Abraham staggered not at the promise of God ... but was strong in faith."

JOHN 20:24-29

24 But Thomas, one of the twelve, called Didymus, was not with them when Jesus came.
25 The other disciples therefore said unto him, We have seen the Lord. But he said unto them, Except I shall see in his hands the print of the nails, and put my finger into the print of the nails, and thrust my hand into his side, I will not believe.
26 And after eight days again his disciples were within, and Thomas with them: then came Jesus, the doors being shut, and stood in the midst, and said, Peace be unto you.
27 Then saith he to Thomas, Reach hither thy finger, and behold my hands; and reach hither thy hand, and thrust it into my side: and be not faithless, but believing.
28 And Thomas answered and said unto him, My Lord and my God.
29 Jesus saith unto him, Thomas, because thou hast seen me, thou hast believed: blessed are they that have not seen, and yet have believed.

Why did Thomas find it hard to believe Jesus was alive? Thomas knew of the nails that pierced Jesus' hands and the spear that was thrust into His side. His physical senses told him Jesus was dead. Thomas was using head knowledge, rather than heart faith.

Compare now the faith of Abraham:

ROMANS 4:17-21

17 (As it is written, I have made thee [Abraham] a father of many nations,) before him whom he believed, even God, who quickeneth the dead, and calleth those things which be not as though they were.
18 Who against hope believed in hope, that he might become the father of many nations, according to that which was spoken, So shall thy seed be.
19 And being not weak in faith, he considered not his own body now dead, when he was about an hundred years old, neither yet the deadness of Sarah's womb:
20 He staggered not at the promise of God through unbelief; but was strong in faith, giving glory to God;
21 And being fully persuaded that, what he had promised, he was able also to perform.

7

Notice the difference in Thomas' faith and Abraham's faith. Thomas had only a natural, human faith which said, "I'm not going to believe unless I can see and feel." Abraham, however, believed God's Word, considering not his own body — his own natural senses. If Abraham didn't consider physical knowledge or feelings, what did he consider? (The Word of God.)

Years ago when I was healed of heart trouble, I was struggling along some of these faith lines that many people do. Alarming heart symptoms would return.

While praying and standing on the promises of God, even while suffering severe pain, the Lord reminded me of Abraham, who *"considered not his own body."* He showed me I should not consider my body, but rather I should consider His Word. As I did this, repeating to myself some of God's promises in the Scriptures regarding healing, such as, *"Himself took our infirmities, and bare our sicknesses,"* every symptom would leave. Too many times we focus our attention on the wrong thing. We consider our physical body and the symptoms rather than looking to God's Word.

In one church I visited, a certain woman regularly ended her testimony with, "You pray for me. I believe I've got cancer." No doubt if she keeps believing it, she will get it. (Jesus said, *"According to your faith be it unto you."*) Another person requested prayer, saying, "Please pray for me. I believe I'm taking a cold." If that is the way you believe, it won't do any good for me to pray, because *"According to your faith be it unto you"* (Matt. 9:29). We need to walk by faith, not by sight.

Some have misunderstood this type of teaching, thinking I tell people to deny all symptoms and go on as if they weren't even there. They think I am teaching Christian Science. However, this is not Christian Science; this is Christian sense. We do not deny pains and other symptoms, for they are very real. Instead, we look beyond them to God's promises.

Real faith in the Word says, "If God says it is so, it is so. If He says, *'By whose stripes ye were healed,'* I am healed. If He says, *'My God shall supply all your need,'* He does. If He says, *'The Lord is the strength of my life,'* He is." In other words, real faith simply says about one's self what the Word says.

Real faith is built on the Word. We should meditate on the Word, dig deeply into it, and feed upon it. Then the Word becomes a part of us, just as natural food becomes a part of our physical body when we eat. What natural food is to the physical man, the Word of God is to the spiritual man. The Word builds confidence and assurance into us.

Memory Text:
"Now faith is the substance of things hoped for, the evidence of things not seen" (Heb. 11:1).

THE LESSON IN ACTION: *"But be ye doers of the word, and not hearers only . . ."* (James 1:22).

8

Lesson 3

Faith vs. Hope

Bible Texts: 1 Corinthians 13:13; Ephesians 2:8,9; Romans 10:9,10,13

Central Truth: It takes a positive faith — a now faith — to get positive results.

When Paul, writing to the Corinthians, said, "And now abideth faith, hope, charity, these three; but the greatest of these is charity" (1 Cor. 13:13), he was not inferring that hope and faith are not important.

Each has its place, and one cannot be substituted for another. We cannot substitute love for hope. Neither can we substitute hope for faith. Yet so many people try to receive things from God on the basis of hope rather than faith.

Faith Is Now

Hope looks to the future. It is always future tense. *Faith is now.* Faith says, "I'll receive the answer right now. I have it now." It is not hoping that gets the job done; it is believing.

Someone said, "Well, I believe I will receive my healing — sometime." That's not faith, that's hope, because it is looking to some indefinite, future time. Faith says, "I receive my healing — now!"

In one modern translation of the New Testament, the familiar verse in Hebrews 11:1 reads, "Faith is giving substance . . . to things hoped for."

If you need healing, you don't want it in the future; you want it right now, especially if you're in pain. If you are seeking the baptism of the Holy Spirit, you want to receive now, not at some indefinite future time. If you need salvation, you cannot put it off to the future, for that may be too late.

I have talked to people who told me they *hoped* to be saved. Some of them are now dead. They left the world unsaved, because salvation that is based on hope never comes to fruition.

EPHESIANS 2:8,9
8 For by grace are ye saved through faith; and that not of yourselves: it is the gift of God:

9 Not of works, lest any man should boast.

ROMANS 10:9,10,13
9 That if thou shalt confess with thy mouth the Lord Jesus, and shalt believe in thine heart that God hath raised him from the dead, thou shalt be saved.

10 For with the heart man believeth unto righteousness; and with the mouth confession is made unto salvation . . .

13 For whosoever shall call upon the name of the Lord shall be saved.

The above verses point man to the plan of salvation. We see that it is by faith — not hope — that we are saved. Jesus promised He will not cast any out who come to Him, but will save all

9

who "*call upon the name of the Lord.*" Therefore, we don't need to *hope* that He will save us. He said He would.

How Do We Get Faith?

Faith, we know, grows out of the Word of God. "*So then faith cometh by hearing, and hearing by the word of God*" (Rom. 10:17). Another translation of this verse reads, "Faith is the warranty deed, that the thing for which you have fondly hoped is at last yours."

Faith is "*the evidence of things not seen,*" as we read in Hebrews 11:1. To illustrate, you might hope for finances to meet a certain obligation, but faith gives you the assurance that you will have the money when you need it. You might hope for physical strength to do a job you must do, but faith says, "*The Lord is the strength of my life*" (Ps. 27:1). In other words, faith says the same thing the Word of God says.

Unbelief is really taking sides against God's Word. There are those who talk unbelief and take sides *against* the Word of God, and then wonder why God's Word doesn't work for them. *If we want God's Word to work for us, we must agree with it.*

Many times when I ask people who come for prayer in my meetings if they believe they will be healed, they answer, "Well, I sure *hope* I will." I tell them they won't, because we receive from God by faith, not hope. Still others answer, "Well, I want to." But I tell them, "You might want a new Cadillac, but that doesn't mean you'll get one. You see, just wanting to won't get the job done."

It's not hoping or wanting: It's faith that gets the job done. You will not receive from God because you hope. Nowhere does the Bible say that when we pray, we shall receive what we hope for. God's Word does say, however, "*. . . What things soever ye desire, when ye pray, BELIEVE that ye receive them, and ye shall have them*" (Mark 11:24). Jesus also said, "*And all things, whatsoever ye shall ask in prayer, BELIEVING, ye shall receive*" (Matt. 21:22). Not hoping, but believing.

Notice in the definition of faith in Hebrews 11:1 ("Now faith is the substance of things hoped for, the evidence of things not seen"), the verb "is" is in the present tense.

Remember, if it's not now, it's not faith. Faith is present tense; hope is future tense. Even though you might say you believe, if you are putting it into the future, you are not believing; you're hoping. In order for it to work, it must be in the correct tense — the present tense. Some people always are believing that God *is going to* do something for them, but faith believes that He *has done,* and *is doing.*

Some years ago while I was preaching in Oklahoma, a woman who hadn't taken a step in four years was brought to the service for prayer. She was in her seventies, and the doctors had said she never would walk again. At the close of the service when we were ready to have prayer for the sick, her friends brought her forward and sat her down on the altar.

I knelt in front of her, laid my hands on her, and prayed. Then I said, "Now arise and walk in the Name of the Lord Jesus Christ."

She did her best to get up, but all the time she was crying and praying, "O dear Jesus, please heal me. Please let me walk. Oh, please . . . please!" She continued in this vein for some time until finally I was able to quiet her enough to talk to her. I asked her, "Sister, did you know that you are healed?"

Astonished, she looked up at me and said, "Oh, am I?"

"Yes," I said, "you are healed, and I will prove it to you from the Bible." Then I opened my Bible to First Peter 2:24, handed it to her, and asked her to read the verse aloud.

She read, *"Who his own self bare our sins in his own body on the tree, that we, being dead to sins, should live unto righteousness: by whose stripes ye were healed."* I asked her to repeat the last phrase, and she read, *". . . by whose stripes ye were healed."*

Then I asked her the question, "Is 'were' past tense, future tense, or present tense?"

"It is past tense," she answered.

"If you *were* healed by Jesus' stripes, then you *are* healed now, aren't you?" I said. A smile spread across her face and her eyes lit up with new understanding. Then I told her, "Just lift your hands and look up to Him. Begin to praise Him because you *are* healed, present tense. Because you *are* healed — not going to be — you *are* . . . now."

With childlike faith she looked up and said, "Dear Lord Jesus, I'm so glad I'm healed." She hadn't walked a step and therefore had no physical evidence of healing whatever. Yet she said, "I'm so glad I'm healed."

I turned to her and said, "Now, my sister, arise and walk in Jesus' Name." Immediately she jumped off that altar like a 16 year old, and walked, leaped, ran, and praised God.

You see, we had to help her get it in the right tense — because faith is present tense. As long as we are struggling to receive, hoping to see the answer sometime, it won't work. That is just hope. Faith says, "It's mine. I have it now."

Hope, of course, used properly is most blessed and beautiful. We have a blessed hope in the soon return of our Lord Jesus Christ, the Resurrection of the righteous dead, the Rapture of the living saints, the hope of heaven, and the hope of seeing our loved ones and friends. We thank God for that hope. But this is all future tense.

Jesus is coming, whether we believe it or not. He is coming because the Word says so. The Resurrection will take place whether we have faith or not. The dead in Christ will rise to meet Him in the air, whether we believe or not. Our faith, or lack of faith, will not affect these events. Jesus is coming back again, because the Word says He will. This is the blessed hope all Christians look forward to.

But it is faith, not hope, that can change the impossible to the possible.

It is faith, not hope, that brings healing and victory.

Hope is a good waiter, but a poor receiver. Too many times I've heard people say, "I'm hoping and praying," or "All we can do now is hope and pray." If that is all you are doing, you're defeated. It takes a positive faith — a *now* faith — to get positive results.

Memory Text:
"And now abideth faith, hope, charity, these three; but the greatest of these is charity" (1 Cor. 13:13).

THE LESSON IN ACTION: *"But be ye doers of the Word, and not hearers only . . ."* (James 1:22).

Lesson 4

Faith Sees the Answer

Bible Texts: Proverbs 4:20-22; Hebrews 13:5,6; 4:14; Mark 11:23

Central Truth: By continually looking at the Word, faith sees the answer.

In our past lessons, we have learned that faith is not something we have as much as it is something we do. We have seen that faith is not *hoping* that we will see the answer in the *future;* faith is *believing* that we have the answer *now*. The eyes of faith see the answer as having already happened.

PROVERBS 4:20-22

20 My son, attend to my words; incline thine ear unto my sayings.
21 Let them not depart from thine eyes; keep them in the midst of thine heart.
22 For they [my words] are life unto those that find them, and health to all their flesh.

Notice that this Scripture says, *"Let them* [my words] *not depart from thine eyes ..."* Many people fail because they see themselves as failing. If they are sick, they think of themselves as dying.

God's Word says, *"Himself* [Jesus] *took our infirmities, and bare our sicknesses"* (Matt. 8:17). If that Word does not depart from before your eyes, you are bound to see yourself without sickness and without disease. You will see yourself as well.

If, however, you do not see yourself as without sickness, then that Word has departed from before your eyes. And even though God wants to make health a reality in your life, He cannot, because you are not acting on His Word.

Notice also the 22nd verse, *"For they* [my words] *are life unto those that find them, and health to all their flesh."* The Hebrew word translated "health" here is also the word for medicine. In other words, "My words are medicine to all their flesh."

The first two verses of this passage tell us the directions for taking this medicine. What are these directions? ("Attend to," or study God's Word, and "keep them in the midst of thine heart," or obey this Word.)

And what is God's medicine? "My words are life unto those that find them, and medicine to all their flesh." But the medicine has to be taken according to directions in order to work. And one of the directions is, *"Let them* [my words] *not depart from thine eyes."* Keep looking at what the Word says.

Too many people pray and pray, but they never see themselves with the answer. They just see everything getting worse. They keep looking at the wrong thing — at the symptoms, at conditions, at themselves — and so they walk in unbelief and destroy the effects of their praying.

Get your mind on the answer. See yourself as having received. Constantly affirm, even in the face of contradictory evidence, that God has heard your prayer because the Word says so. That's when you'll get results.

You have to believe you've got it before you can receive it. *"What things soever ye desire, when ye pray, believe that ye receive them, and ye shall have them"* (Mark 11:24). The believing comes *before* the receiving.

There are those who say, "I'm not going to believe anything I can't see." But in the natural we believe a lot of things we can't see. The whole world became alarmed when atomic bombs were being exploded, releasing radioactive material into the atmosphere. You can't see it or feel it, but it is a destructive power nevertheless.

Faith Contradicts Circumstances

HEBREWS 13:5,6
5 ... for he hath said, I will never leave thee, nor forsake thee.
6 So that we may boldly say, The Lord is my helper, and I will not fear what man shall do unto me.

Are we boldly saying that the Lord is our Helper? That is what we should be saying.

"Well, you all pray for me, I feel as if the Lord has forsaken me," cried one poor sister. "I don't know if I can make it or not. I hope I can. Pray for me that I'll hold out faithful to the end." This is a familiar request in prayer and testimony meetings. But that is not what God told us to say!

Too many people are boldly saying,

"I'm whipped, I'm defeated. The devil's got me bound." But nowhere in the Bible do we find where God said to boldly say that.

God said, *"I will never leave thee, nor forsake thee. So that we may boldly say, The Lord is my helper."*

Let's quit saying the wrong thing and start saying the right thing. Say the Lord is your Helper. Say that the Lord is your Healer. Say that the Lord took your infirmities and bore your sicknesses. Keep talking about the right thing. Keep believing the right thing.

Wrong thinking, wrong believing, and wrong talking will defeat you. The devil can't defeat you, because Jesus already has defeated the devil *for* you. Satan doesn't defeat you; you defeat yourself. Or if he does, you permit him to do so. It is a consent of ignorance.

God has given us His Word to direct us so our believing will be right. If our thinking is right and our believing is right, our talking will be right. "The Lord is my helper." "The Lord is my strength."

Faith 'Says' the Answer

Real faith in the Word says that if God says it is so, it's so. If He says *"... by whose stripes ye were healed"* (1 Peter 2:24), we are healed. If He says, *"My God shall supply all your need according to his riches in glory by Christ Jesus"* (Phil. 4:19), He does it. If the Word says, *"... the Lord is the strength of my life"* (Ps. 27:1), He is.

14

In other words, real faith in God simply says about one's self what the Word says. We have what the Word says we have. We are what the Word says we are. If God says we are strong, we are. If He says we are healed, we are. If He says He cares for me, He does.

HEBREWS 4:14
14 Seeing then that we have a great high priest, that is passed into the heavens, Jesus the Son of God, let us hold fast our profession.

Because Jesus is our High Priest and sits at the right hand of God in heaven, making intercession for us, we can have the answers to our petitions now. Looking up the Greek word translated "profession," I learned that it should read, "Let us hold fast to saying the same things."

Jesus is in heaven, representing us at the throne of God. He is saying, "I took their place, I died for them as their Substitute." Jesus didn't die for Himself. He didn't need to redeem Himself, because He wasn't lost. He died for us. He became our Substitute. He took our sins. He bore our sicknesses and carried our diseases. He died for us, arose from the dead for us, and ascended on high for us. He is up there now saying, "I did that for them," and we are to hold fast to saying the same things down here.

MARK 11:23
23 ... whosoever shall say unto this mountain, Be thou removed, and be thou cast into the sea; and shall not doubt in his heart, but shall believe that those things which he saith shall come to pass; he shall have whatsoever he saith.

It isn't just a matter of faith going out of your heart toward God without your saying anything. That won't work. Nowhere in the Bible do we read that we should do that.

Faith *kept only in your heart* never will bring healing to your body, the infilling of the Holy Spirit, or an answer to prayer. But faith in your heart *released through your lips* will bring results.

Memory Text:
"Let them [my words] *not depart from thine eyes ..."* (Prov. 4:21).

THE LESSON IN ACTION: *"But be ye doers of the word, and not hearers only ..."* (James 1:22).

Lesson 5

Faith in Action (Part 1)

Bible Texts: Joshua 6:2-5,16,20; Luke 5:18-20,24,25

Central Truth: Great miracles are wrought by those who act upon God's Word.

In both the Old and New Testaments we see examples of how God's people, by putting their faith into action, were able to accomplish mighty deeds. Great miracles were wrought by humble men who acted upon God's Word in simple believing faith.

Faith in Action in the Old Testament

JOSHUA 6:2-5,16,20

2 And the Lord said unto Joshua, See, I have given into thine hand Jericho, and the king thereof, and the mighty men of valour.
3 And ye shall compass the city, all ye men of war, and go round about the city once. Thus shalt thou do six days.
4 And seven priests shall bear before the ark seven trumpets of rams' horns: and the seventh day ye shall compass the city seven times, and the priests shall blow with the trumpets.
5 And it shall come to pass, that when they make a long blast with the ram's horn, and when ye hear the sound of the trumpet, all the people shall shout with a great shout; and the wall of the city shall fall down flat, and the people shall ascend up every man straight before him ...
16 And it came to pass at the seventh time, when the priests blew with the trumpets, Joshua said unto the people, Shout; for the Lord hath given you the city ...
20 So the people shouted when the priests blew with the trumpets: and it came to pass,

when the people heard the sound of the trumpet, and the people shouted with a great shout, that the wall fell down flat, so that the people went up into the city, every man straight before him, and they took the city.

In verse two we read that God told Joshua He had given the city of Jericho "into thine hand." This didn't mean, however, that Joshua and the children of Israel could sit back and relax while the city automatically became theirs. They had to *do* something.

God gave them explicit instructions how to go about possessing the land He already had given them, but they had to *believe* that Word and *act* upon it. Their acting upon the Word was their faith in action.

They were to march around the walls of the city once a day for six days. On the seventh day, they were to march around the city seven times. Then, when the musical instruments sounded, they were to shout.

Notice that they shouted *while the walls were still up!* Anybody can shout when the walls are down — it doesn't take any faith to do that. But they *acted* their faith. They "shouted with a great shout," and the walls fell down!

Too many people are sitting back waiting for something to come to them. They are more or less inert, with a passive faith instead of an active faith, waiting for something to happen.

I met a man like this years ago in Colorado. He had no job. He had a wife and five children, and he was just waiting for something to turn up. But the only thing that turned up was more bills. He needed to get busy. We all have certain obligations. We can't just stay at home and expect something to come to us. But if we pray, believe, and then act, something will happen.

Faith in Action in the New Testament

LUKE 5:18-20,24,25

18 And, behold, men brought in a bed a man which was taken with a palsy: and they sought means to bring him in, and to lay him before him.
19 And when they could not find by what way they might bring him in because of the multitude, they went upon the housetop, and let him down through the tiling with his couch into the midst before Jesus.
20 And when he saw their faith, he said unto him, Man, thy sins are forgiven thee . . .
24 . . . I say unto thee, Arise, and take up thy couch, and go into thine house.
25 And immediately he rose up before them, and took up that whereon he lay, and departed to his own house, glorifying God.

While Jesus was in a house teaching, some men brought their friend to Him to be healed. The man had palsy and was bedfast. The crowd was so large that these men could not get to Jesus. But rather than give up, they determined to find some way to get their friend to Him. They climbed onto the roof and through an opening in the tiling they lowered the bedfast man into the room before the Lord.

By whose faith was this miracle brought about: the man on the cot, or the friends who brought him to the Lord? The Scripture says, "And when he saw THEIR faith . . ." The word "their" is plural. It was the faith of all of them. It would have been easy for the man's friends, upon seeing the great throng surrounding Jesus, to have shrugged their shoulders, given up, and gone back home, saying, "Well, at least we tried. We did the best we could." But they didn't give up that easily. They found a way to get their friend to Jesus.

The sick man demonstrated great faith, too, because how many invalids would allow themselves to be carried up on a rooftop? Furthermore, when Jesus told him to rise and walk, he wasn't any better. He lay there just as helpless as ever. He could have said, "Rise and walk? Why, didn't you see these men carry me in here? I can't possibly get up. You'll have to heal me first." But, no, when Jesus told him to rise, he began to move, and when he did, healing was the result. If he had refused to act on the word of the Master, he would not have received healing. But because he *acted*, he *received*.

Faith in Action in the Twentieth Century

In the early days of the Pentecostal movement, a woman evangelist was ministering to four people in wheelchairs. In a very quiet voice she said, "Rise and walk in Jesus' Name." Three of these people got up and walked. The fourth said, "I can't walk."

"The others couldn't walk either," the evangelist said, "but they did."

"I know they did," the crippled woman answered, "but I can't. You see, I haven't walked in years." And the evangelist had to walk away and leave her sitting there. The others acted their faith and reaped the results.

In one church where I was ministering, there was a man who had been burned over the lower part of his body, leaving him unable to walk. He just scooted his feet along on the floor. During the healing service one evening, this man came forward for prayer. The Lord had told me what to do, and when I came to him I asked him, "Can you run?"

Astonished at such a question, he said, "Oh, no, I can't even walk, much less run."

Then I said, "The Lord has told me to tell you to run." The man didn't even give it a second thought. He just turned and started scooting up the aisle as fast as he could. He scooted around the church in this manner three or four times, and by the time he got back to the front, he was walking normally. He was perfectly healed! He had acted his faith.

In the service the next night we saw another miracle as the result of the first. Two elderly gentlemen responded to the invitation — something which is not often seen.

I learned later that these men were brothers, ages 72 and 74, who lived next door to the man who had been healed the night before. When they saw their crippled neighbor out working in his yard the next day, they thought he had crawled out there. But then they saw him get up, straight and well, and walk around the house. They hurried over to find out what had happened. He told them about his healing and what the Lord had done for him. As a result, both men came to the service that night and gave their hearts to the Lord.

One of the best definitions of faith is: *If you believe, you will act.* If you believe God's Word, you will act as if it is true. *"Now faith is the substance of things hoped for, the evidence of things not seen"* (Heb. 11:1). Faith is giving substance to the thing hoped for.

Memory Text:
"Now faith is the substance of things hoped for, the evidence of things not seen" (Heb. 11:1).

THE LESSON IN ACTION: *"But be ye doers of the word, and not hearers only ..."* (James 1:22).

Faith in Action (Part 2)

Bible Texts: Acts 19:1-6; 1 Corinthians 14:14

Central Truth: The formula of faith in action can apply to receiving the baptism of the Holy Spirit just as it does to receiving any of God's gifts.

In the previous lesson we talked about how faith is an action; it puts God's Word into practice. Many miracles of healing have come about as people have acted on their faith, stepped out on God's promises, and received from God.

The same thing applies to receiving the baptism of the Holy Spirit. In order to receive this mighty enduement of God's power, we also must step out in faith and lay claim to the promises of the Father.

The Gift of the Holy Spirit: Already Given

ACTS 19:1-6

1 And it came to pass, that, while Apollos was at Corinth, Paul having passed through the upper coasts came to Ephesus: and finding certain disciples,
2 He said unto them, Have ye received the Holy Ghost since ye believed? And they said unto him, We have not so much as heard whether there be any Holy Ghost.
3 And he said unto them, Unto what then were ye baptized? And they said, Unto John's baptism.
4 Then said Paul, John verily baptized with the baptism of repentance, saying unto the people, that they should believe on him which should come after him, that is, on Christ Jesus.

5 When they heard this, they were baptized in the name of the Lord Jesus.
6 And when Paul had laid his hands upon them, the Holy Ghost came on them; and they spake with tongues, and prophesied.

As we study the Book of Acts, we notice that after the Day of Pentecost, the disciples always asked believers the question, "Have you received the Holy Ghost?" They didn't say, "Has God given you the Holy Ghost?" God is not going to *give* you the Holy Ghost. As far as He is concerned, He already has. It is up to you to *receive*. It is something you do yourself.

Some say, "I just wish it were as easy to receive the baptism of the Holy Spirit as you make it sound."

But just how difficult is it to receive a gift? If a man were to ask me for a book which I held, I would hand it to him. I would be giving him a gift of the book. But suppose he were then to start crying and begging, "Please, oh, please, Brother Hagin. Please give it to me!" Of course, people would think he was crazy. They would wonder why he didn't just reach out and take it.

Spiritual things are just as real as material things. God offers us the gift of the Holy Spirit. We don't have to cry and beg for it. God says, "Here is the gift of the Holy Spirit. If you are born again, you can receive now. You don't have to wait; you're ready now to receive the Holy Spirit!" *"So then faith cometh by hearing, and hearing by the word of God"* (Rom. 10:17). We have His promise in the Word. Faith is acting on the Word.

During a meeting which I was conducting in a town in Texas, a woman came forward for prayer to receive the Holy Spirit. I laid hands on her and prayed, the Holy Spirit came upon her, but she wouldn't respond. I laid hands on her a second time and prayed, but again she wouldn't respond. I opened my Bible to Acts 2:4 and asked her to read that verse of Scripture aloud. She read, *"And they were all filled with the Holy Ghost, and began to speak with other tongues, as the Spirit gave them utterance."*

"Who does the Scripture say did the speaking in tongues?" I asked.

"It says the Holy Spirit did," she answered.

I told her to read it again. Finally, after reading it four times, she saw what she had missed before. Astonished, she looked at me and said, "Why, *they* did the speaking in tongues! I had always thought that the Holy Spirit did the speaking."

Then I said, "Let's read several other Scriptures, too," and I pointed her to Acts 10:44-46: *"While Peter yet spake these words, the Holy Ghost fell on all them which heard the word. And they of the circumcision which believed were astonished, as many as came with Peter, because that on the Gentiles also was poured out the gift of the Holy Ghost. For they heard them speak with tongues, and magnify God."*

We then turned to Acts 19:6, *"And when Paul had laid his hands upon them, the Holy Ghost came on them; and they spake with tongues, and prophesied."*

"Now I want to ask you a question," I said. "When I laid hands on you earlier, did the Holy Spirit come upon you? Did you feel the power of God upon you?"

"Absolutely," she said.

"Did your tongue want to say something that wasn't English?" I asked.

"Why," she said, "it was all I could do to keep from it."

"You're not supposed to keep from it," I said. "You're supposed to cooperate with it." (Some people seem to think that they are supposed to fight against that urge as long as they can and finally be overpowered by the Spirit. When the Holy Spirit gives you utterance, you must have faith to act.)

Some time ago I was talking to a fellow who had been tarrying for some 15 years. He said, "You can't tell me one thing about tarrying. I know all about seeking God." He knew all about *seeking* but nothing about *receiving*. And there is a great deal of difference between the two.

A minister friend of mine told me about a man who said to him, "I've been seeking the Holy Spirit for 19 years."

20

The minister replied, "You haven't done any such thing. Jesus said, *'Seek, and ye shall find'* (Matt. 7:7). If you had been seeking, you would have found. All you've been doing is just hanging around the altar." It seems that this is all that many are doing — just hanging around the altar. It's time to quit hanging around and start acting on the Word of God, because faith is acting.

The Gift of the Holy Spirit: A Spiritual Experience

1 CORINTHIANS 14:14
14 For if I pray in an unknown tongue, my spirit prayeth, but my understanding is unfruitful.

Your body is the temple or house of your own spirit. When you become born again, the Holy Spirit comes to dwell in your spirit. Therefore, your body then becomes the temple of the Holy Spirit.

The baptism of the Holy Spirit is an experience subsequent to the New Birth. Receiving this baptism of the Holy Spirit is a *spiritual* experience, not a *mental* or a *physical* experience.

You cannot contact God with your mind. God is not a mind. Numbers 23:19 says, *"God is not a man ..."* This means God is not a physical being. He is a spirit.

Notice that He is not "spirit," but He is *"a spirit."* The word "spirit" to many people means an influence or an atmosphere. But God is not spirit. Jesus said, *"God is a Spirit ..."* (John

4:24). He is a divine personality. We cannot contact God with our minds; we cannot contact Him with our bodies. We contact God with our spirits, because He is a spirit.

This is where many people have difficulty in trying to receive the Holy Spirit. They try to receive the Holy Spirit mentally or physically. They want a *physical* experience, but it is a *spiritual* experience. The only physical part of it is the actual speaking in tongues. He will give you utterance, but that utterance comes out of *your* spirit, and *you* speak the words.

Paul said, *"For if I pray in an unknown tongue, my spirit prayeth, but my understanding is unfruitful"* (1 Cor. 14:14). *The Amplified Bible* reads, "My spirit [by the Holy Spirit within me] prays." In other words, it is the Holy Spirit within you who gives you the ability to speak with other tongues.

Jesus said, *"And I will pray the Father, and he shall give you another Comforter, that he may abide with you for ever"* (John 14:16). He comes in to live and dwell in you, and you must learn to respond to Him. He will give you the utterance. Many people fail here because they rely on their natural senses — what they can see, hear, or feel. They will not believe they have the Holy Spirit until they speak with tongues. However, you believe and receive the Holy Spirit first; then you speak with tongues as a result of having received.

"And they were all filled with the Holy Ghost ..." (Acts 2:4). Notice this

Scripture says they were filled. Then, after they were filled, they began to speak with other tongues. This is the very thing that many people stumble over. They want to talk in tongues *first* and *then* believe that they have the Holy Spirit. But you have to believe *first*.

In order to receive the gift of the Holy Spirit, just as to receive anything from God, you have to step out in faith, putting your faith to work. Then you will have faith in action.

Memory Text:
". . . The Holy Ghost came on them; and they spake with tongues, and prophesied" (Acts 19:6).

THE LESSON IN ACTION: *"But be ye doers of the word, and not hearers only . . ."* (James 1:22).

Faith vs. Feelings

Bible Texts: John 20:24-29; 2 Corinthians 5:17

Central Truth: A formula for faith is: (1) Find a promise in God's Word for whatever you are seeking. (2) Believe God's Word. (3) Do not consider contradictory circumstances. (4) Praise God for the answer.

The beloved man of faith Smith Wigglesworth once said, "I can't understand God by feelings. I can't understand the Lord Jesus Christ by feelings. I can only understand God the Father and Jesus Christ by what the Word says about them. God is everything the Word says He is. We need to get acquainted with Him through the Word."

Too many people try to get acquainted with God through their feelings. When they feel good, they think God has heard their prayers. When they don't feel particularly good, they think He has not heard them. Their faith is based on their feelings, whereas it should be based on God's Word.

A 'Thomas' Faith

JOHN 20:24-29

24 But Thomas, one of the twelve, called Didymus, was not with them when Jesus came.

25 The other disciples therefore said unto him, We have seen the Lord. But he said unto them, Except I shall see in his hands the print of the nails, and put my finger into the print of the nails, and thrust my hand into his side, I will not believe.

26 And after eight days again his disciples were within, and Thomas with them: then came Jesus, the doors being shut, and stood in the midst, and said, Peace be unto you.

27 Then saith he to Thomas, Reach hither thy finger, and behold my hands; and reach hither thy hand, and thrust it into my side: and be not faithless, but believing.

28 And Thomas answered and said unto him, My Lord and my God.

29 Jesus saith unto him, Thomas, because thou hast seen me, thou hast believed: blessed are they that have not seen, and yet have believed.

Thomas was one who based his faith upon his feelings. He said he would not believe unless he could *see* with his own eyes the prints of the nails in Jesus' hands, and *touch* these nailprints with his own hands. He relied on what he could see and touch, not on what God had to say.

We have many "Thomas Christians" today — those who believe only what they can feel, see, hear, or touch. Real faith in God is based upon the Word of God. Real faith says, "If God says it is true, it is." Believing God is believing His Word. If God's Word says He hears me, I know He hears me, because His Word cannot lie.

If our faith is based upon feelings,

we are just using natural human faith, and we cannot get spiritual results with natural human faith. We have to use scriptural faith — Bible faith — believing in God's Word.

Once I prayed for a woman who had been through many healing lines, but she never had received her healing. After I prayed, she immediately said, "I haven't got it yet. Pray again." I prayed again, and when I was finished, she said the same thing.

After praying a third time with seemingly no results I asked her, "When are you going to start believing you are healed?"

"Well," she said, "when I get healed."

"What in the world would you want to believe it for, then? It seems to me that you would know it then," I told her.

Anyone can believe what he can feel, hear, or see. We live and operate in the physical realm most of the time, and obviously we have to walk by sight *then.* But when it comes to Bible things — to spiritual things — we don't walk by sight; we walk by faith.

Healing Is Spiritual

God's healing is spiritual healing. If medical science heals, it heals through the *physical.* Christian Science heals through the *mind.* But when God heals, He heals through the *spirit.*

2 CORINTHIANS 5:17
17 Therefore if any man be in Christ, he is a new creature: old things are passed away; behold, all things are become new.

Spiritual healing, or divine healing, is received from God in the same way that the New Birth, which is a rebirth of the spirit, is received.

When you are born again, it is not your body that is born again, because you still have the same body you always had. When Paul said, *"Therefore if any man be in Christ, he is a new creature . . .,"* he was not talking about man's body being made new. The New Birth doesn't change the physical in any way. After you are saved, the man on the inside is to dominate the physical, of course, but it is this inner man who is born again.

The New Birth is the rebirth of the human spirit. Jesus said, *"That which is born of the flesh is flesh; and that which is born of the Spirit is spirit"* (John 3:6). We cannot tell immediately just what has happened on the inside of a person, because it takes place in the human spirit. But if a person walks in the light of what he has, in the process of time it will become obvious.

We often were mistaken when we saw people come to the altar, pray, cry, jump up, and hug everyone, acting so happy. Then they were never seen again. We really thought they had received something marvelous from God, but it was just an emotional experience, not the New Birth.

At other times we saw people come to the altar for salvation who were not emotional at all. We wondered if they had received anything from the Lord. We thought they were not at the altar long enough for anything. Yet many of these became outstanding Christians during their lifetimes. (This is another example of faith based on physical senses.)

I certainly believe in feeling, but I put it last. God's Word comes first, faith in God's Word second, and feeling last. Too many people turn it around and put feeling first, faith in their feelings second, and the Word of God last. These people never will make a success of anything.

Walking in the natural, we do have to go by our physical senses. (For example, if we are crossing a street and our eyes tell us cars are coming, we must wait until they pass.) But too many people try to believe in God with that physical, natural faith, and if their physical senses tell them it's not so, they believe it's not so. Our physical senses have nothing to do with the Bible. God's Word is true, regardless of our feelings or the circumstances: *"For ever, O Lord, thy word is settled in heaven"* (Ps. 119:89).

Formula for Faith

Here is a formula for faith that you can make work for you:

First, have God's Word for whatever you may be seeking; *second,* believe God's Word; *third,* refuse to consider the contradictory circumstances, or what your physical senses may tell you about it; and, *fourth,* give praise to God for the answer.

Follow these four steps, and you always will get results. These are four certain steps to deliverance, healing, answered prayer, or whatever you may be seeking from the Lord.

Memory Text:
"For ever, O Lord, thy word is settled in heaven" (Ps. 119:89).

THE LESSON IN ACTION: *"But be ye doers of the word, and not hearers only ..."* (James 1:22).

Lesson 8

What It Means To Believe With the Heart (Part 1)

Bible Texts: 1 Thessalonians 5:23; Romans 12:1,2; Luke 16:19-25

Central Truth: Man is a spirit; he has a soul; and he lives in a body.

For years I searched for a satisfactory explanation of what it means to believe with the heart. I read Mark 11:23, which says, *"For verily I say unto you, That whosoever shall say unto this mountain, Be thou removed, and be thou cast into the sea; and shall not doubt in HIS HEART, but shall believe that those things which he saith shall come to pass; he shall have whatsoever he saith."*

Romans 10:10 also talks about believing with the heart: *"For WITH THE HEART man believeth unto righteousness . . ."*

The word "heart" used in these Scriptures does not refer to the physical organ that pumps blood through our body and keeps us alive. That would be believing God with our body. We couldn't believe with our physical heart any more than we could believe with our physical hand or finger. The word "heart" is used to convey a thought.

Notice how we use the word "heart" today. When we talk about the heart of a tree, we mean the center, the very core. When we talk about the heart of a subject, we mean the most important part of that subject, the very center of it, the main part around which the rest revolves. And when God speaks of man's heart, He is speaking about the main part of man, the very center of his being, which is the spirit.

Man Is a Spirit

1 THESSALONIANS 5:23
23 And the very God of peace sanctify you wholly; and I pray God your whole SPIRIT and SOUL and BODY be preserved blameless unto the coming of our Lord Jesus Christ.

The terms "spirit of man" and "heart of man" are used interchangeably throughout the Bible. We know that man is a spirit, because he is made in the image and likeness of God, and Jesus said, *"God is a Spirit . . ."* (John 4:24).

Thus, it is not our physical bodies that are like God, for the Bible says that God is not a man. Remember, there is an inward man and an outward man. Man is a *spirit;* he has a *soul;* and he lives in a *body.*

Paul said in his letter to the Romans, *"For he is not a Jew, which is one outwardly; neither is that circumcision, which is outward in the flesh: But he is a Jew, which is one inwardly; and CIRCUMCISION IS*

THAT OF THE HEART, IN THE SPIRIT, and not in the letter; whose praise is not of men, but of God" (Rom. 2:28,29). According to this text, the heart is the spirit.

Speaking to Nicodemus, Jesus said, *"Ye must be born again"* (John 3:7). Nicodemus, being human, could think only in the natural; therefore, he asked, *"How can a man be born when he is old? can he enter the second time into his mother's womb, and be born?"* (v. 4). Jesus answered, *"That which is born of the flesh is flesh; and that which is born of the Spirit is spirit"* (v. 6). The New Birth is a rebirth of the human spirit.

In John's Gospel we also read where Jesus told the woman at the well in Samaria, *"God is a Spirit: and they that worship him must worship him in spirit and in truth"* (John 4:24). We cannot contact God with our body or with our mind. We can contact God with our spirit.

First Corinthians 14:14 says, *"For if I pray in an unknown tongue, my spirit prayeth, but my understanding is unfruitful."* The spirit is not the mind. Some people mistakenly think that the mind is the spirit. However, as this verse indicates, we know that when we speak in tongues, this does not come from our mind, or our own human thinking, but from our spirit — from our innermost being — from the Holy Spirit within our spirit. Paul went on to say, *"What is it then? I will pray with the spirit, and I will pray with the understanding also . . ."* (v. 15). In other words, Paul was saying that his spirit is the real Paul.

The Inward Man

Paul also said, *"For which cause we faint not; but though our outward man perish, yet the inward man is renewed day by day"* (2 Cor. 4:16). Paul pointed out that there is an outward man and an inward man. The outward man is the body. The inward man is the spirit. And the spirit has a soul.

In First Corinthians 9:27 Paul said, *"But I keep under my body, and bring it into subjection: lest that by any means, when I have preached to others, I myself should be a castaway."* If the body were the real man, Paul would have said, "I keep myself under; I bring myself into subjection." He refers to his body as "it." "I" is the man on the inside, the inward man who has been reborn. We do something with our body: We bring it into subjection. The man we look at is not the real man; it is just the house we live in.

We can now more easily understand Paul's writings to the saints at Rome:

ROMANS 12:1,2

1 I beseech you therefore, brethren, by the mercies of God, that ye present your bodies a living sacrifice, holy, acceptable unto God, which is your reasonable service.

2 And be not conformed to this world: but be ye transformed by the renewing of your mind, that ye may prove what is that good, and acceptable, and perfect, will of God.

In this epistle, Paul was not writing to unbelievers, but to Christians. He addresses his letter *"To all* that be in Rome, beloved of God, called to be saints..." (Rom. 1:7). Although he was writing to men and women who had been born again, he said they needed to do something with their bodies and their minds.

The New Birth is not a rebirth of the human *body*, but a rebirth of the human *spirit*. And the infilling of the Holy Spirit is not a physical experience, but a spiritual experience.

Paul said we have to present our bodies to God a living sacrifice.

We have to get our minds renewed with the Word.

Notice that this is something that we do — not God. God gives eternal life. He offers us His Spirit. But God doesn't do anything with our bodies. If anything is done with them, we have to do it.

The Word says that *you* present your body unto God. Nobody else can do it for you. The Word says that *you* are to be "*transformed by the renewing of your mind.*" Our minds are renewed through the Word of God.

We know that man is a spirit, made in the image and likeness of God. Some people believe that man is just an animal. However, if that were true, it wouldn't be any more wrong to kill a man and eat him than it would be to kill a cow and eat it! Man has a physical body that he is living in, but he is not an animal. He is more than just mind and body. He is spirit, soul, and body. He is a spirit; he has a soul; and he lives in a body.

Animals have souls, but they are not spirits. There is nothing in animals

that is like God.

God took something of Himself and put it in man. He made the body of man out of the dust of the earth, but He breathed into man's nostrils the breath of life.

The word "breath," or *ruach* in the Hebrew, means breath or spirit, and is translated "Holy Spirit" many times in the Old Testament. God is a spirit, so He took something of Himself — spirit — and put it into man. When He did, man became a living soul. He wasn't alive until then. He became a living soul. He became conscious of himself, because the body was dead without the spirit.

The soul possesses intellectual and emotional qualities, and animals have souls. But when their physical bodies are dead, they are dead.

Human souls — our intellectual and emotional qualities — are not based upon the physical, but upon the spirit; and when our body is dead, our soul still exists.

LUKE 16:19-25

19 There was a certain rich man, which was clothed in purple and fine linen, and fared sumptuously every day:

20 And there was a certain beggar named Lazarus, which was laid at his gate, full of sores,

21 And desiring to be fed with the crumbs which fell from the rich man's table: moreover the dogs came and licked his sores.

22 And it came to pass, that the beggar died, and was carried by the angels into Abraham's bosom: the rich man also died, and was buried;

23 And in hell he lift up his eyes, being in

torments, and seeth Abraham afar off, and Lazarus in his bosom.

24 And he cried and said, Father Abraham, have mercy on me, and send Lazarus, that he may dip the tip of his finger in water, and cool my tongue; for I am tormented in this flame.

25 But Abraham said, Son, remember that thou in thy lifetime receivedst thy good things, and likewise Lazarus evil things: but now he is comforted, and thou art tormented.

In this passage of Scripture we have a very vivid illustration of man's three parts: spirit, soul, and body. Notice verse 22 says, *"the beggar died, and was carried by the angels into Abraham's bosom."* Who was carried away? (The beggar. Not his body, but *he*.) His spirit is the real person. His body was put in the grave, but he was in "Abraham's bosom."

The rich man also died. His body was put in the grave, but *"in hell he lift up his eyes."* Although Abraham's body had been in the grave many years, the rich man saw *him.* He also recognized Lazarus. Therefore, in the spirit realm, man looks very similar to what he does in this life.

The rich man cried out to Abraham, *". . . have mercy on me, and send Lazarus, that he may dip the tip of his finger in water, and cool my*
tongue; for I am tormented in this flame. But Abraham said, Son, remember. . . ."*

Man is a spirit, and he has a soul. We see in this Scripture that his soul is still intact. He can still remember. He has emotion. He was tormented. He was concerned about his five brothers still living (vv. 27,28).

God is a spirit. He became a man, for Jesus was God manifested in the flesh, living in a human body. He took on a physical body, and when He did, He was no less God than He was before.

We know that man leaves his physical body at death, and when he does he is no less man than he was when he had his physical body, as proved by the story of the rich man and Lazarus.

We cannot know God through our human knowledge — through our mind. God is only revealed to man through his spirit. It is the spirit of man that contacts God, for God is a spirit.

Memory Text:
"For with the heart man believeth unto righteousness; and with the mouth confession is made unto salvation" (Rom. 10:10).

THE LESSON IN ACTION: *"But be ye doers of the word, and not hearers only . . ."* (James 1:22).

What It Means To Believe With the Heart (Part 2)

Bible Texts: 2 Corinthians 5:1,6-8; Proverbs 3:5-7

Central Truth: To believe with all of our heart is to believe with our spirit, independently of our mind or our body.

Spiritual things are just as real as material things. God is just as real as if He had a physical body, although He doesn't. He is a spirit.

Jesus has a physical body now — a flesh-and-bone body — but not flesh and blood. After His resurrection, He appeared to the disciples, and they thought He was a spirit (or ghost). But Jesus said, *"handle me . . . for a spirit hath not flesh and bones . . ."* (Luke 24:39).

On another occasion, while Peter and some of the other disciples were fishing, they saw Jesus on the shore. He called them, and they went to Him and ate fish He was cooking on an open fire.

He has a physical body now — a resurrected flesh-and-bone body. And Jesus, who is now in heaven with His physical body, is not *more* real than the Holy Spirit or God the Father are real.

Notice we do not say God is spirit, but rather that God is a spirit. Some people think that God is spirit, meaning some sort of an impersonal influence. Even though we say that God is a spirit, that doesn't mean He doesn't have a shape or a form in the spiritual realm, because He does.

Angels are spirits, yet angels have a form, or a spirit body.

On one occasion when the Israelites were surrounded by the Syrian army, the servant of the prophet Elisha was filled with fear as he saw the enemy's host of horses and chariots which compassed the city. Elisha merely answered, *"Fear not: for they that be with us are more than they that be with them. And Elisha prayed, and said, Lord . . . open his eyes, that he may see. And the Lord opened the eyes of the young man; and he saw: and, behold, the mountain was full of horses and chariots of fire round about Elisha"* (2 Kings 6:16,17). Sometimes, as God wills, angels can take on a form in the material realm where they can be seen.

In Exodus 33 we read that God talked to Moses *"face to face"* (v. 11), although Moses did not see God's face, because a cloud was there. *"Thou canst not see my face: for there shall no man see me, and live"* (v. 20).

Then God said to Moses, *"And it shall come to pass, while my glory passeth by, that I will put thee in a clift of the rock, and will cover thee with my hand while I pass by: And I will take away mine hand, and thou shalt see my back parts: but my face shall not be seen"* (vv. 22,23).

Even though God is a spirit, we know that He has a face and hands — a form of some kind. He is no less real because He is a spirit than He would be if He had a physical body. Spiritual things are just as real as material things.

2 CORINTHIANS 5:1,6-8
1 For we know that if our earthly house of this tabernacle were dissolved, we have a building of God, an house not made with hands, eternal in the heavens. . . .
6 Therefore we are always confident, knowing that, whilst we are at home in the body, we are absent from the Lord:
7 (For we walk by faith, not by sight:)
8 We are confident, I say, and willing rather to be absent from the body, and to be present with the Lord.

When our body is put in the grave, we still have a building with God that is not made with hands, and we shall live eternally in the heavens. Who is going to be absent from the body? *We* are — the real man — the inward man.

In First Peter 3:4 our spirit is called *"the hidden man of the heart."* Here we see the word "heart" again. The inward man — our spirit — is called the hidden man. He is a man of the heart, of the spirit. He is hidden to the physical or the natural man. In Romans 7:22 the spirit is called the "inward man." (*"For I delight in the law of God after the inward man."*) So we see this "inward man" and the "hidden man" give us God's definition of the human spirit.

The real man is spirit; he has a

body and a soul. With his *spirit* he contacts the spiritual realm. With his *soul* he contacts the intellectual realm. With his *body* he contacts the physical realm.

We cannot contact God with our mind. Neither can we contact God with our body. We can contact God only with our spirit.

The Word of God — Key to Heart Faith

When we hear the Word of God preached, we hear it with our natural mind. (Before we were Christians, the Holy Spirit, through the Word, spoke to our heart or our spirit.) We read in First Corinthians 2:14, *"The natural man receiveth not the things of the Spirit of God . . ."* One translation says, "The natural man or the natural mind understandeth not the things of the Spirit of God, for they are foolishness unto him. Neither can he know them because they are spiritually discerned."

We don't understand the Bible with our mind. It is spiritually understood. We understand it with our spirit, or our heart. That is the reason we may read certain passages dozens of times and never understand their true meaning. Then one day we suddenly see what God is showing us through His Word. It is at that moment that we understand it with our heart. We have to get the revelation of God's Word in our heart. That is why we must depend upon the Spirit of God to open and unveil the Word to us.

31

Therefore, to believe with the heart means to believe with the spirit. How does our spirit get faith that our intellect cannot obtain? The answer is: through the Word.

When Jesus said, *"... Man shall not live by bread alone, but by every word that proceedeth out of the mouth of God"* (Matt. 4:4), He was speaking of spiritual food. He used a natural term to convey a spiritual thought.

Our spirit becomes filled with assurance and confidence as we meditate on the Word. The Word is spirit and faith food. The Word of God is food that makes our spirit strong.

To believe with the heart means to believe apart from what our physical body may tell us, or what our physical senses may indicate. This is because the physical man believes what he sees with his physical eyes, hears with his physical ears, or feels through his physical senses. But the spirit, or heart, believes in the Word regardless of seeing, hearing, or feeling.

PROVERBS 3:5-7
5 Trust in the Lord with all thine heart; and lean not unto thine own understanding.
6 In all thy ways acknowledge him, and he shall direct thy paths.
7 Be not wise in thine own eyes: fear the Lord, and depart from evil.

Most people practice verse 5 all right, but they practice it in reverse. They trust with all their understanding and lean not to their own heart! James 1:19 says, *"... let every man be swift to hear, slow to speak, slow to wrath."* This is another verse

we are inclined to practice in reverse. We are swift to speak and swift to wrath, but slow to hear.

Then verse 7 in the above passage of Scripture says, *"Be not wise in thine own eyes ..."* In other words, "Don't be wise with natural human knowledge, which would cause you to act independently of the Word of God."

In the New Testament we find the counterpart of this Scripture. *"(For the weapons of our warfare are not carnal, but mighty through God to the pulling down of strong holds;) Casting down imaginations* [reasoning], *and every high thing that exalteth itself against the knowledge of God, and bringing into captivity every thought to the obedience of Christ"* (2 Cor. 10:4,5).

Peace — A Result of Heart Faith

If we want to walk by faith, the Word must be uppermost to everything else. And as we trust God with all our heart, a quietness and a peace come to our spirit. *"For we which have believed do enter into rest ..."* (Heb. 4:3). *"And the peace of God, which passeth all understanding, shall keep your hearts and minds through Christ Jesus"* (Phil. 4:7). *"Thou wilt keep him in perfect peace, whose mind is stayed on thee: because he trusteth in thee"* (Isa. 26:3).

God's Word says, *"But my God shall supply all your need according to his riches in glory by Christ Jesus"* (Phil. 4:19). We know in our spirit that everything we need will be supplied. We don't worry. We have no anxiety. If we are worrying, we are not believing. Our heart takes courage as we read the Word. As we meditate in this Word, our assurance becomes deeper. This assurance in our spirit is independent of human reasoning or human knowledge. It may even contradict human reasoning or physical evidence. *But to believe God with our heart means to believe apart from our body.*

Dr. Lilian Yeomans said, "God delights in His children stepping out over the aching void with nothing underneath their feet but the Word of God."

The reason why many people are defeated is because they accept defeat. But God's Word says, *"Ye are of God, little children, and have overcome them: because greater is he that is in you, than he that is in the world"* (1 John 4:4). The Holy Spirit rises up in us, and we know we cannot be conquered. We know because we *believe!*

Memory Text:
"Trust in the Lord with all thine heart; and lean not unto thine own understanding" (Prov. 3:5).

THE LESSON IN ACTION: *"But be ye doers of the word, and not hearers only ..."* (James 1:22).

33

Confession: Key To Unlocking Faith

Bible Texts: Matthew 3:5,6; John 16:7-11; Matthew 10:32,33

Central Truth: Confessing the lordship of Jesus Christ is the very heart of the Gospel.

Few Christians realize the place that confession holds in God's scheme of things. And it is to be regretted that whenever we use the word "confession," people invariably think of confessing sins, weaknesses, and failings. That is the negative side of confession. There is a positive side, and the Bible has more to say about the positive aspects of confession than the negative!

The dictionary says that to confess means "to acknowledge or to own, to acknowledge faith in." To confess, according to the dictionary, means to make confession of one's faults, but it also says it means to make confession of one's faith.

There are four kinds of confessions spoken of in the New Testament: (1) the teachings of John the Baptist and Jesus regarding confession of sins of the Jews; (2) the confession of the sinner today; (3) the believer's confession of his sins when he is out of fellowship with God; and (4) the confession of our faith in God's Word.

Confession of Sins of the Jews

It is important to make the distinction between the sins of the Jews under the first covenant, to whom Jesus and John the Baptist were talking in Scripture, and the sins of the unbeliever today who has never met Christ.

MATTHEW 3:5,6
5 Then went out to him Jerusalem, and all Judaea, and all the region round about Jordan,
6 And were baptized of him in Jordan, confessing their sins.

Here we see the picture of God's covenant people confessing their sins and being baptized by John. *This was not Christian baptism.* Jesus had not died and risen.

John did not baptize in the Name of the Father, the Son, and the Holy Spirit. He baptized only in the Name of the Father. These people were Jews under the law.

Confession of the Sinner Today

JOHN 16:7-11
7 Nevertheless I tell you the truth; It is expedient for you that I go away: for if I go not away, the Comforter will not come unto you; but if I depart, I will send him unto you.
8 And when he is come, he will reprove the world of sin, and of righteousness, and of judgment:

9 Of sin, because they believe not on me;
10 Of righteousness, because I go to my Father, and ye see me no more;
11 Of judgment, because the prince of this world is judged.

Notice the words of Jesus in verse 9: *"Of sin, because they believe not on me."* Jesus shows us that the sinner will be convicted by the Holy Spirit of only one sin, and that is *"because they believe not on me."*

How many times have we insisted that the sinner confess all the sins he has ever committed in order to be saved. However, he couldn't confess *all* the sins he has ever committed. He couldn't *remember* everything he has ever done! The chief confession the sinner must make is the lordship of Jesus.

In Acts 19:18 we read, *"And many that believed came, and confessed, and shewed their deeds."* These were Gentiles. It doesn't say what they confessed, but it is evident from the verse that follows that they were confessing the magical arts they had been practicing. *"Many of them also which used curious arts brought their books together, and burned them before all men ..."* (v. 19). They were not confessing these things to get saved, because they already were saved. They gave them up *because* they were now saved.

So many times people have gotten the cart before the horse. They tell unsaved people, "You are going to have to quit this, and you're going to have to give up that before you can get saved." But the main issue is that they accept the lordship of Jesus. Then those other things will take care of themselves.

In the last church I pastored, there was a family in which the wife was saved but the husband wasn't. When I visited in the home and invited the husband to come to church, he said, "No, I don't want to come to church, because when I do, I feel uneasy. I get under conviction. Just this morning my wife asked me why I didn't give up this and that and get saved. She doesn't know it, but for weeks at a time I have tried giving up these things, but I always go back to them. I've tried and failed. There's no use in my coming to church. I just can't live it."

Here is an example of confession in reverse. He was trying to clean up his life and quit all his habits — he was trying to do it all himself — so he could get saved. But what he should have done was just confess the lordship of Jesus. *"That if thou shalt confess with thy mouth the Lord Jesus, and shalt believe in thine heart that God hath raised him from the dead, thou shalt be saved"* (Rom. 10:9).

The sinner has served Satan. He is guilty of only one sin in the sight of God: the rejection of Jesus Christ as Savior and Lord. God demands that the sinner confess the lordship of Jesus. Confessing the lordship of Jesus is the very heart of the Gospel.

To demand that a sinner confess his sins *before* God can make him a new creature makes no more sense than it would for the governor of a state to say to a convict in prison, "I will parole you if you will confess that you are in prison." It is a self-evident fact that he is in prison.

Likewise, it is self-evident that the sinner is a child of the devil. What he must confess is the lordship of Christ. He must be truly sorry for the sins of the past and turn from them, forsaking them completely and acknowledging his need of a Savior. Then he must let Jesus dominate his daily life.

Notice also the words, *"Thou shalt confess with thy mouth ..."* There must be a vocal confession. The lips must frame the words. Confession is not only for our sakes, but it is also for the sake of the world and for the sake of Satan, who has ruled our lives.

While I was conducting a meeting in Dallas, Texas, a number of years ago, some men in the church came to me asking prayer for a certain man who still was unsaved, although he had been coming to their early morning prayer services five days a week for six months.

I met him a few nights later at a Saturday night Bible class I was conducting especially for men who worked and couldn't attend our day sessions. The Lord immediately spoke to my heart and showed me what the problem was. We had a few testimonies in this meeting, and then I asked this man to stand and give his testimony. Startled, he stammered, "Why, I can't. I'm not saved yet."

I asked him to turn in his Bible to Romans 10:9,10 and read these verses aloud. He read, *"That if thou shalt con-* *fess with thy mouth the Lord Jesus, and shalt believe in thine heart that God hath raised him from the dead, thou shalt be saved. For with the heart man believeth unto righteousness; and with the mouth confession is made unto salvation."* When I asked him to read the last phrase again, he repeated, *"And with the mouth confession is made unto salvation."*

I said, "Certainly you can't be saved until you confess. It is with the mouth that confession is made unto salvation, according to the Scripture which you have just read. Now stand and confess that you are saved."

"But I don't *feel* that I am saved," he replied.

"Maybe not," I said, "but you have been coming to this church early every morning for six months praying to be saved."

"Yes, I have repented and prayed, cried and begged God for forgiveness," he said.

"Then all you lack is standing on this verse," I said.

Somewhat reluctantly he stood and said, "Well, I do believe these verses that Jesus died for my sins and was raised from the dead, and that God raised Him up for my justification. So I take Him as my Savior and confess Him as my Lord." Then he quickly sat down.

To direct attention away from him, I called on another man to testify. Several others testified as well. Glancing back at him, I noticed his face was shining with the glory of God. I turned to him and said, "Now would you like to testify again?"

He leaped to his feet and said, "When I made that statement — when I confessed Jesus as my Lord — something happened inside of me," and he went on to praise the Lord joyfully.

I told him, "Most assuredly something happened to you! Eternal life was imparted to your spirit."

Confession in Public

MATTHEW 10:32,33
32 Whosoever therefore shall confess me before men, him will I confess also before my Father which is in heaven.
33 But whosoever shall deny me before men, him will I also deny before my Father which is in heaven.

Notice in these verses Jesus states our confession must be public. Public confession is really a break with the world. It defines our position. It shows our change of lordship. The confession of the lordship of Jesus puts us immediately under His supervision, care, and protection. Before this, Satan was our lord, but now Jesus is our Lord. Not only do we confess this to ourselves and to the world, but we confess it to the devil. In this way we overcome his hold on us and have victory through Jesus.

Memory Text:
"For with the heart man believeth unto righteousness; and with the mouth confession is made unto salvation" (Rom. 10:10).

THE LESSON IN ACTION: *"But be ye doers of the word, and not hearers only..."* (James 1:22).

Lesson 11

Confession Restores Broken Fellowship

Bible Texts: Psalm 137:1-4; 1 John 1:3-10; James 5:14,15; Hebrews 10:1-4

Central Truth: Faith has no song when fellowship is broken.

In our studies on the subject of confession, we have covered the first two types: the confession of the sins of the Jews, and the confession of the sinner today.

In this lesson we will deal with the confession of a believer who is out of fellowship with God.

In Psalm 137 we see a dramatic example of broken fellowship. As a result of sin, Israel had been carried away into Babylon.

PSALM 137:1-4
1 By the rivers of Babylon, there we sat down, yea, we wept, when we remembered Zion.
2 We hanged our harps upon the willows in the midst thereof.
3 For there they that carried us away captive required of us a song; and they that wasted us required of us mirth, saying, Sing us one of the songs of Zion.
4 How shall we sing the Lord's song in a strange land?

In this passage of Scripture, Israel laments her captivity. God's people remember Zion, but they are now in sorrow, and their harps are hung on the willows. They cannot *"sing the Lord's song in a strange land."*

Faith cannot sing when fellowship is broken. We lose our testimony the moment we sin. Sin always puts the light out.

Confession Brings Forgiveness

1 JOHN 1:3-10
3 That which we have seen and heard declare we unto you, that ye also may have fellowship with us: and truly our fellowship is with the Father, and with his Son Jesus Christ.
4 And these things write we unto you, that your joy may be full.
5 This then is the message which we have heard of him, and declare unto you, that God is light, and in him is no darkness at all.
6 If we say that we have fellowship with him, and walk in darkness, we lie, and do not the truth:
7 But if we walk in the light, as he is in the light, we have fellowship one with another, and the blood of Jesus Christ his Son cleanseth us from all sin.
8 If we say that we have no sin, we deceive ourselves, and the truth is not in us.
9 If we confess our sins, he is faithful and just to forgive us our sins, and to cleanse us from all unrighteousness.
10 If we say that we have not sinned, we make him a liar, and his word is not in us.

Many use these verses only when dealing with the unsaved. However, they were written to the believer, and they should only be used in connection with Christians who are out of fellowship with God because of sin in their lives.

Notice that the word "fellowship" is mentioned four times in these verses. They were written to the believer, not the sinner, first, as a warning against broken fellowship; and second, to show the way back into fellowship with the Lord.

Verse 6 says, *"If we say that we have fellowship with him, and walk in darkness, we lie, and do not the truth."* In other words, if we are out of fellowship and declare that we are all right, we are not telling the truth.

But He says that if we will confess our sins, He is *"faithful and just to forgive us our sins, and to cleanse us from all unrighteousness."*

One point we should make clear here is that if you have sinned, you will know it.

The instant you do wrong, something on the inside of you will tell you. Your recreated spirit will instantly let you know you have committed sin. If you miss the mark in some way, do not wait. Stop right then and ask the Lord's forgiveness. He will forgive, and you may continue walking in fellowship with Him.

Forgiveness Restores Fellowship

When you confess your sins, He forgives you at that moment and you stand in His presence as though you never had sinned. It is not necessary to keep confessing these same sins over and over again, because this builds weakness, doubt, and sin-consciousness into the spirit.

If you confessed it once, He forgave you and He forgot it. He has no memory of it: *"I, even I, am he that blotteth out thy transgressions for mine own sake, and will not remember thy sins"* (Isa. 43:25). And in Jeremiah 31:34 we read, *". . . for I will forgive their iniquity, and I will remember their sin no more."*

If God has no memory of the sin that broke your fellowship with Him, why should you? It is not the Holy Spirit who is convicting you. It is Satan trying to take advantage of you.

Psalm 103:1-3 says, *"Bless the Lord, O my soul: and all that is within me, bless his holy name. Bless the Lord, O my soul, and forget not all his benefits: Who forgiveth all thine iniquities; who healeth all thy diseases."*

Sometimes people ask me to pray for them and say, "I don't know if the Lord will hear me or not, because I sinned and failed." However, if they have asked God's forgiveness, He doesn't remember that they have done anything wrong. So why should they remember it? They have needlessly talked themselves right out of faith. The believer also must be willing to forgive *himself* just as God is willing to forgive him. Too many people have robbed themselves of faith because they are not willing to forgive themselves.

Forgiveness in Healing

JAMES 5:14,15

14 Is any sick among you? let him call for the elders of the church; and let them pray over him, anointing him with oil in the name of the Lord:

15 And the prayer of faith shall save the sick, and the Lord shall raise him up; and if he have committed sins, they shall be forgiven him.

These verses often are used in connection with prayer for healing, and rightly so. But let us not overlook the last part — *"and if he have committed sins, they shall be forgiven him."*

Many times when we see someone become ill whom we know to be out of fellowship with the Lord, we think, *He has done wrong; now he's going to reap the results of his wrongdoing. He is sick because of his sin.* Sometimes broken fellowship will cause sickness, but the Word of God says, *". . . and if he have committed sins, they shall be forgiven him."*

I have known people who thought they had to lie on the bed of sickness indefinitely because they had failed and sinned. This is not necessary, however. The Scripture says, *"And the prayer of faith shall save the sick, and the Lord shall raise him up; AND IF HE HAVE COMMITTED SINS, THEY SHALL BE FORGIVEN HIM."* There *is* forgiveness in healing.

HEBREWS 10:1-4

1 For the law having a shadow of good things to come, and not the very image of the things, can never with those sacrifices which they offered year by year continually make the comers thereunto perfect.

2 For then would they not have ceased to be offered? because that the worshippers once purged should have had no more conscience of sins.

3 But in those sacrifices there is a remembrance again made of sins every year.

4 For it is not possible that the blood of bulls and of goats should take away sins.

This is the story of the failure of the blood of bulls and goats to *take away* sin. Their blood could only *cover* it. It left the sin in the hearts of men. And with the sin was sin-consciousness.

But in our redemption in Christ, God has redeemed us from sin-consciousness. *"If we confess our sins, he is faithful and just to forgive us our sins, and to cleanse us from all unrighteousness"* (1 John 1:9).

You should have no more knowledge of your sin. God doesn't; why should you? You can see with what confidence and boldness you can come in prayer, knowing with a certainty that He hears you.

Memory Text:
"If we confess our sins, he is faithful and just to forgive us our sins, and to cleanse us from all unrighteousness" (1 John 1:9).

THE LESSON IN ACTION: *"But be ye doers of the word, and not hearers only . . ."* (James 1:22).

40

Confession of God's Word Builds Faith

Bible Texts: Mark 16:15-20; Isaiah 41:10; Psalm 119:28,130; Mark 11:23

Central Truth: Confession is faith's way of expressing itself. Faith's confession creates reality.

It is always possible to tell if a person is believing right by what he says. If his confession is wrong, his believing is wrong. If his believing is wrong, his thinking is wrong. If his thinking is wrong, it is because his mind has not been renewed with the Word of God.

All three — believing, thinking, saying — go together. God has given us His Word to get our thinking straightened out. We can think in line with God's Word.

In our studies on the subject of confession we have dealt with three types of confession: the confession of the sins of the Jews, the confession of the sinner today, and the confession of a believer who is out of fellowship with God. In this lesson we will discuss the confession of our faith in God's Word.

As we mentioned in the previous lesson, whenever the word "confession" is used, we instinctively think of sin and failure. But that is the negative side. It is important in its place, of course, but there is a positive side, and the Bible has more to say about the positive than the negative.

Confession is stating something we believe in our hearts. It is giving evidence to something we know to be true. It is testifying to a truth we have accepted.

Confession's Five Parts

Our confession should center around five things:

(1) What God has done for us in the plan of redemption.

(2) What God has done *in us,* through His Word and His Spirit.

(3) What we are to the Father in Christ Jesus.

(4) What Jesus is accomplishing for us now at the Father's right hand, where He is making intercession for us.

(5) What God can accomplish *through* us.

Confession at Work — Preaching the Word

MARK 16:15-20

15 And he said unto them, Go ye into all the world, and preach the gospel to every creature.

16 He that believeth and is baptized shall be saved; but he that believeth not shall be damned.

17 And these signs shall follow them that believe; In my name shall they cast out devils; they shall speak with new tongues;
18 They shall take up serpents; and if they drink any deadly thing, it shall not hurt them; they shall lay hands on the sick, and they shall recover.
19 So then after the Lord had spoken unto them, he was received up into heaven, and sat on the right hand of God.
20 And they went forth, and preached every where, the Lord working with them, and confirming the word with signs following.

God works through us by His Word through our lips. Jesus said, *"Go ye into all the world, and preach the gospel to every creature."* That is the way God works through us.

We carry the Word to the lost. If we do not carry the Word to the world, then we waste our time praying for God to do something. In other words, it would be useless to pray for someone who is lost if we do not carry the Gospel of salvation to him.

If we could just pray and get people saved, we wouldn't have to send missionaries all over the world. We could just pray all the heathen into the kingdom. However, the Holy Spirit works only in connection with the Word.

In obedience to Christ's command to go into all the world and preach, the disciples went forth preaching the Word everywhere, and the Lord worked with them, confirming the Word with signs following. God didn't do a thing until the disciples preached the Word. Then signs followed.

Signs don't follow an individual; they follow the Word. Give the Word out and the signs will take care of themselves. You don't follow signs. Signs follow the Word.

In the last church I pastored, I became greatly concerned that there weren't enough signs following my ministry. I shut myself away in prayer for several days asking God for more signs.

Finally the Lord spoke to me and said, "You have been praying that I would confirm my word and that signs would follow. But all you have to do is to preach the Word and I will confirm it. If you will preach the Word, signs will follow. If the signs aren't following, you are not preaching the Word."

I was startled by this, but upon closer examination of my preaching, I discovered it was true. I had mingled a lot of tradition and personal opinion into my sermons. And God won't confirm tradition with signs following.

As I began preaching more and more of the undiluted Word of God, I began to see more signs following. The more Word I preached, the more signs I had!

God moves only in line with His Word. He has magnified His Word above His Name. And we cannot expect to get help from God if we are taking sides against His Word, even though it may be an unconscious act on our part.

We should treat the Word of God with the same reverence we would show to Jesus if He were present in the natural.

Confession Dispels Fear

ISAIAH 41:10

10 Fear thou not; for I am with thee: be not dismayed; for I am thy God: I will strengthen thee; yea, I will help thee; yea, I will uphold thee with the right hand of my righteousness.

Have you ever noticed, in reading the Bible, how many times God told His children "fear not"?

When Jairus sought Jesus to heal his daughter, the Lord said to him, *"FEAR NOT: believe only, and she shall be made whole"* (Luke 8:50). When Jesus was preaching to His disciples, He said, *"FEAR NOT, little flock; for it is your Father's good pleasure to give you the kingdom"* (Luke 12:32).

When the Lord appeared to Isaac in the Old Testament, renewing the covenant He had made with his father Abraham, the Lord said, *"FEAR NOT, for I am with thee, and will bless thee . . ."* (Gen. 26:24).

If God had just said, "Don't be afraid," and had left us there, we might say, "But I can't help being afraid." But not only did He say "fear not"; He also said, "I am with thee." Can we really believe He is with us and still be afraid? No, if we are afraid, it is because we are doubting Him.

"But," someone might say, "I am so weak." God said, "I will strengthen thee."

"But I am so helpless," someone else might say. God said, "I will uphold thee."

PSALM 119:28,130

28 My soul melteth for heaviness: strengthen thou me according unto thy word. . . .
130 The entrance of thy words giveth light; it giveth understanding unto the simple.

It is true that in ourselves we may be weak and helpless, burdened down with cares and problems. But in our weakness we look to His Word for strength, for *"The entrance of thy words giveth light; it giveth understanding unto the simple."*

Our confession can be, "God is with me." We can say, "Greater is he that is in me than he that is in the world" (1 John 4:4) and "If God be for me, who can be against me?" (Rom. 8:31).

You may be facing some problem that seems impossible. Instead of talking about how impossible it is, look to Him who is inside you and say, "God is in me now." You'll find your confession of faith will cause Him to work in your behalf. He will rise up in you and give you success.

The Master of Creation is in you! You can face life fearlessly because you know that greater is He who is in you than any forces that may be arrayed against you. This should be your continual confession.

Confession Increases Faith

There is no faith without confession. Confession is faith's way of expressing itself.

Faith, like love, is of the heart — of the spirit. And we know there is no love without word or action. We cannot reason love into people, nor can we reason love out of them. It is of the heart. As faith, too, is of the spirit or

43

heart, we can safely say that there is no faith without confession. *Faith grows with confession.*

The confession of the believer does two things for him. First, it identifies him. Second, it sets the boundaries of his life. *He never will have more than his confession.*

MARK 11:23

23 For verily I say unto you, That WHO-SOEVER SHALL SAY unto this mountain, Be thou removed, and be thou cast into the sea; and shall not doubt in his heart, but shall BELIEVE THAT THOSE THINGS WHICH HE SAITH shall come to pass; HE SHALL HAVE WHATSOEVER HE SAITH.

If we say we can't do something, then of course we can't. But if we say we can, then we can. According to Mark 11:23, we can have whatever we say or confess, whether it be belief or unbelief, success or failure, sickness or health.

The reason the majority of Christians, although sincere, are weak is because they never have dared to make a confession of who and what they are in Christ. They must find out how God looks at them and then confess it.

These privileges are found mostly in the New Testament epistles, because they were written to the Church. When you discover all that God has for you, boldly confess what the Word declares you are in Christ. As you do this, your faith will abound.

The reason faith is held in bondage is because you never have dared confess what God says you are.

Remember, *faith never grows beyond your confession.* Your daily confession of what the Father is to you, of what Jesus is doing for you now at the right hand of the Father, and of what His Holy Spirit is doing in you will build a solid, positive faith life.

You will not be afraid of any circumstances. You will not be afraid of any disease. You will not be afraid of any conditions. You will face life fearlessly, a conqueror. And to be a conqueror you must confess you are one: *"Nay, in all these things we are more than conquerors through him that loved us"* (Rom. 8:37).

Looking again at the key Scripture in Romans 10:10, we see in capsule form God's law of faith: *"For with the heart man believeth unto righteousness; and with the mouth confession is made unto salvation."*

In seeking anything from God, you first must *believe* in your heart, because the Word said it. Then you must *confess* with your mouth that it is so.

For example, to be saved, a man must *believe* in his heart and *confess* with his mouth that Jesus died for him according to the Scriptures and was raised from the dead for his justification. Third, he will *receive* (or see) the answer to his prayer.

Believe it; confess it; receive it. *"Whosoever . . . shall BELIEVE that those things which he SAITH shall come to pass; he SHALL HAVE WHATSOEVER HE SAITH"* (Mark 11:23).

As you study God's Word and

learn what His Word says you are, who you are, and what you have in Christ Jesus, even though it may not seem real to you at first, start confessing, "Yes, that's mine, according to God's Word."

You will then find that *faith's confession creates reality.*

Memory Text:
"For verily I say unto you, That whosoever shall say unto this mountain, Be thou removed, and be thou cast into the sea; and shall not doubt in his heart, but shall believe that those things which he saith shall come to pass; he shall have whatsoever he saith" (Mark 11:23).

THE LESSON IN ACTION: *"But be ye doers of the word, and not hearers only . . ."* (James 1:22).

Lesson 13

Confession of the Believer's Privileges in Christ

Bible Texts: 2 Corinthians 5:17; Ephesians 1:7,8; Acts 17:28

Central Truth: When we know what we are in Christ and think in line with that — when we believe and confess that — there can be no failure for us.

We briefly touched on confession's five parts in our last lesson, but we will go into more detail on these in our study for today as we endeavor to learn more about what we are to confess. Our confession centers around these five things:

(1) What God in Christ has wrought for us in His plan of redemption.

(2) What God, through the Word and the Holy Spirit, has wrought for us in the New Birth and the infilling of the Holy Spirit.

(3) What we are to God the Father in Christ Jesus.

(4) What Jesus is doing for us now at the right hand of the Father, where He ever lives to make intercession for us.

(5) What God can do through us, or what His Word can do through our lips.

Discovering Our Privileges in Christ

As we have said, confession is testifying to something we know. It is impossible to testify to something we *don't* know. And it is what we know

personally about the Lord Jesus Christ and what we are in Him that counts.

First, we can know Him personally. It is of primary importance to be born again. But just because someone has been born again does not necessarily mean he is a successful Christian. He also must know what he is in Christ Jesus. When we know what we are in Him, think in line with that, believe and confess it, there is no failure for us.

To discover what we are in Christ, we must look to the Word of God. Go to the New Testament, primarily the epistles written to the Church, and underline with a red pencil every Scripture that has the expression "in Him," "in Christ," or "in whom." Better yet, take several sheets of paper and write down all of these Scriptures.

The moment you find them, begin to confess that this is who you are and what you have in Christ. If you will do this, I guarantee that your life will be different after just a few days.

While neither time nor space permits us to go into all these Scriptures, let us look at a few.

2 CORINTHIANS 5:17

17 Therefore if any man be in Christ, he is

a new creature: old things are passed away; behold, all things are become new.

Notice the expression "in Christ." What a revolutionary thing that is for believers to believe and confess!

We are new creatures in Christ Jesus. We are not just forgiven sinners. We are not poor, weak, staggering, sinning, barely-getting-along church members.

We are new creatures, created by God in Christ Jesus. We are new creatures with the life of God, the nature of God, and the ability of God in us!

At the age of 17, as a new Christian, I never had the problems so many have, because I was quick to tell everybody, "I am a new creature." I was quick to witness to Christ's saving grace in my life wherever I went. I found that the more I talked about it, the more real the new creation became to me, because that is who and what we are.

I was active in soul-winning — preaching in jail services, on the streets and working in the church.

While I was standing on the street corner one day, a boy I knew came up to me and asked me to do him a favor.

"I wouldn't ask you to do this," he explained, "but I'm running late now and I promised my girlfriend that I would bring a date for her cousin who is visiting from out of town. Would you come along and help me out? I'll always be grateful, and I'll promise that we won't stay over 30 or 40 minutes, and that we won't have any smoking, drinking, or dancing while

you're there." Reluctantly I went along to help him out.

When we got to this girlfriend's house, she introduced me to her cousin. We had barely gotten seated when they put a record on the phonograph and started dancing. When the girl's cousin asked me to dance, I said, "No thank you. I don't dance."

She looked at me as if I had just come from Mars and said, "You don't dance? Why?"

"Because I'm a new creature," I answered.

"What do you mean, you're a new creature?" she asked.

I quoted Second Corinthians 5:17 to her. *"Therefore if any man be in Christ, he is a new creature: old things are passed away; behold, all things are become new."* I said, "There was a time when I was interested in things like dancing, but now my life is different. I have been made a new creature in Christ, with new interests and new desires."

While the record continued to play and the other couple was dancing, I continued to give the girl my testimony of faith in Christ. The words began to grip her heart with conviction, and she started crying. When the record stopped, the boy saw what was happening. He turned to me and said, "Let's go!" and took me right home.

It didn't matter where I was — whether in the jails, on the streets, at school or church — I was quick to witness to everyone I came in contact with that I had been born again and was a new creature in Christ Jesus. And if we will confess that, it will make a big difference in our lives. I wasn't tempted by the things of the world, because I constantly confessed that I was a new creature in Christ Jesus.

Redemption from the Curse of the Law

EPHESIANS 1:7,8
7 In whom we have redemption through his blood, the forgiveness of sins, according to the riches of his grace;
8 Wherein he hath abounded toward us in all wisdom and prudence.

Notice the words, *"In whom we have redemption ..."* How thankful we can be that we are not *trying* to get it; we already *have* it. We are not going to have it sometime; we have it now.

Satan's dominion has been broken. He lost his dominion over our lives the moment we became new creatures. We received a new Lord. Jesus Christ reigns over us. Satan was our lord, but now Jesus is our Lord. (Romans 10:9 says, *"That if thou shalt confess with thy mouth the Lord Jesus ..."* or "Jesus as Lord.") Satan's dominion ended, and Jesus' dominion began the moment we accepted Him as Lord and were born again.

From what and from whom are we redeemed? When asked this question, many people say, "I am redeemed from sin." And that is part of the answer, but not nearly all of it. Galatians 3:13 says, *"Christ hath redeemed us from the curse of the law, being*
made a curse for us: for it is written, Cursed is every one that hangeth on a tree." We are redeemed from the curse of the law.

To find out just what the curse of the law is, we must go back to the first five books of the Bible. There we see that the curse or the punishment for breaking God's law is threefold: poverty, sickness, and the second death.

God has redeemed us from the curse of poverty, the curse of sickness, and the curse of death — spiritual death now and physical death when Jesus comes again. We need have no fear of the second death.

ACTS 17:28
28 For in him we live, and move, and have our being ...

What a vast storehouse of power we overlook so many times! In Christ our Savior and Lord, we have life, energy, and strength for impossible tasks. It does not say that we can do these things in ourselves. It is through Him — through His power — because it is *"in him we live, and move, and have our being."*

Deliverance from the Power of Satan

Then let us look at two Scriptures that, although they do not contain the words "in Him," "in whom," or "in Christ," nevertheless convey something of the same message of what we have in Him.

"Who [God] *hath delivered us from the power of darkness, and hath*

translated us into the kingdom of his dear Son" (Col. 1:13). This verse says we are delivered from the authority of darkness; from the power of Satan.

"Ye are of God, little children, and have overcome them: because greater is he that is in you, than he that is in the world" (1 John 4:4). The Old Testament counterpart to this Scripture is Isaiah 41:10: *"Fear thou not, for I am with thee: be not dismayed; for I am thy God: I will strengthen thee; yea, I will help thee; yea, I will uphold thee with the right hand of my righteousness."*

Then in the New Testament we find, *"What shall we then say to these things? If God be for us, who can be against us?"* (Rom. 8:31). We can take this as a personal message for ourselves. Because we are under the New Covenant, we can say, "Thank God, He is in us." This is the best reason I can think of for not being afraid.

One woman said to me, "But it isn't so in my life. I know it is not."

I replied, "God says it is so; you say it isn't. Therefore, either you or God is lying. If you were to stand before your mother and call her a liar, you would feel bad, wouldn't you? How can you expect to feel right when you stand before God and say, 'Your Word is not true. It isn't so. You're a liar'? To remedy this situation, you must start confessing that His Word *is* so, whether you feel like it is so in your life or not. Then it will become a reality."

We must get our thinking in line with God's Word, and then our believing will be right. When our believing is right, we can confess — say, affirm, witness, testify — to what God's Word says about us. Then we will succeed. Then life will be different for us!

Memory Text:
"For in him we live, and move, and have our being . . ." (Acts 17:28).

THE LESSON IN ACTION: *"But be ye doers of the word, and not hearers only . . ."* (James 1:22).

Right and Wrong Confession

Bible Texts: 2 Timothy 1:7; 1 Peter 2:24; Matthew 8:17

Central Truth: The confession of our lips will give either God or Satan dominion over us.

The Bible is the Word of God and contains God's thoughts. And, of course, God's thoughts are different from man's thoughts.

"For my thoughts are not your thoughts, neither are your ways my ways, saith the Lord. For as the heavens are higher than the earth, so are my ways higher than your ways, and my thoughts than your thoughts" (Isa. 55:8,9).

As we study God's Word and know His thoughts, we can dare to think God's thoughts after Him as we get our thinking in line with His Word!

Studying about confession, we learned that if our confession is wrong, it is because our believing is wrong. If our believing is wrong, it is because our thinking is wrong. And if our thinking is wrong, it is because our mind has not yet been renewed with the Word of God.

Sometimes the teachings of the Word of God may not seem reasonable to the natural man, but that is because his mind has not been renewed by the Word.

Mark 11:22-24 says, *"... Have faith in God* [or the God-kind of faith]. *For verily I say unto you, That whosoever shall say ... and shall not doubt in his heart, but shall believe ...*

shall have whatsoever he saith. Therefore I say unto you, What things soever ye desire, when ye pray, believe that ye receive them, and ye shall have them."

In *The Amplified Bible,* verse 24 reads, "For this reason I am telling you, whatever you ask for in prayer, believe — trust and be confident — that it is granted to you, and you will [get it]."

The greatest things that will ever happen to the Christian will be when he moves out into the spiritual realm. His intellect and physical senses will fight him every step of the way to keep him from entering that realm, because if the natural mind is not renewed by the Word of God, it wants to hold him in the natural realm. But there is a spiritual realm, and this is really the realm of the Christian.

Right and Wrong Confession

Looking into the matter of wrong thinking, wrong believing, and wrong confessing, let us ask the question: Just what is a wrong confession?

Wrong confession is a confession of defeat and failure and the supremacy of Satan. Talking about how the devil is keeping you from success, holding you in bondage, or keeping you sick is a confession of defeat. And such a confession simply glorifies the devil.

As we have said in previous lessons, confession is witnessing for a truth that we have embraced, testifying of something we know, and affirming something we believe. Many times our confessions admit defeat and glorify the devil rather than witness to what God's Word has to say about a matter.

Few of us are like the dear old sister who stood in church to testify, "The devil has been after me all week, *bless his holy name.*" Yet many of our testimonies do more to witness to the supremacy of Satan in our lives than to Christ's dominion!

When we testify to what God has done for us, we glorify Him; by the same token, when we talk about what the devil is doing, and we list our failures and defeats, we glorify the devil. Many people lose the blessing that God has for them just by making a wrong confession. They are defeated, and life becomes a grind to them.

Actually, a confession that glorifies the devil is an unconscious declaration that God is a failure! Such a confession destroys our faith and holds us in bondage. The confession of Satan's ability to hinder and keep us from success gives him dominion over us.

Therefore, with your mouth you either give God or Satan dominion over you. The confession of your lips that has grown out of faith in your heart will absolutely defeat the devil in every combat.

When we are saved, we confess the lordship of Jesus. He begins to have dominion over us and rule in our lives. But when we confess Satan's ability to hinder and keep us from success — even though we may be Christians — we are giving Satan dominion over us. He is the god of this world, and he will move right in, because we permitted him to do so. Even though it may be a permission of ignorance or an unconscious consent, it is nevertheless consent. And when Satan has dominion, we are filled with weakness and fear.

Overcoming Fear and Doubt

2 TIMOTHY 1:7

7 For God hath not given us the spirit of fear; but of power, and of love, and of a sound mind.

Even though we sometimes may feel afraid in the natural, we never should confess fear. Fear is not of God. The above Scripture says that God has not given us a spirit of fear, *"but of power, and of love, and of a sound mind."*

Fear is not something that comes from inside you. It is something that comes from outside, trying to get hold of you. It is from the enemy. We should not confess fear; rather, we should confess power, love, and a sound mind.

The same thing is true of doubt. Don't confess your doubts. This is not to say that you should not admit doubts if you have them. Just don't say anything about them. Doubt is of the devil. Doubt is contraband goods. Doubt is evil. The Christian has no business talking about doubt, because it doesn't belong to him.

Many people think they are being honest when they confess that they doubt. You may have been tempted to doubt, but you can put the devil on the run by resisting him.

So don't confess doubt; confess faith. Start talking about who you are and what you are in Christ. You are a believer. You are a new creature. Talk that; believe that; think that. And if you are tempted — and none of us is above temptation — *"Resist the devil, and he will flee from you"* (James 4:7). Refuse in the Name of the Lord Jesus Christ to doubt, and it will leave you.

Confessing God's Word

Instead of confessing doubts and fears, confess what God's Word says. God said, *"Fear thou not; for I am with thee ..."* (Isa. 41:10). Therefore, you can say, "I am not afraid. I am a child of God, and He is with me. He has not given me a spirit of fear, but of power, and of love, and of a sound mind. I am not a doubter; I am a believer."

Stop talking the devil's language of doubt and fear. Start talking God's language of faith. God is a faith God. We are faith children of a faith God.

In one of my meetings a woman told me about her sister, who was in a mental institution. She said, "She is not too bad, but she does need institutional care. She understands what is said to her. Occasionally I can bring her home for two-week periods. I am going to bring her home now so she can attend these meetings. I believe they will help her."

I never prayed for the sick woman during those two weeks, but she was in every service. Just from hearing the Word, her mind became clear and she never had to return to the institution. The doctors released her, giving her a clean bill of health. In the past she had been confessing defeat, fear, and doubt until they had become a part of her. But as she listened to the Word preached, she saw where she had missed it. She began to confess the right thing, and she was healed.

Seeing the remarkable recovery of this woman, another woman in the church was inspired to bring her neighbor, who was about to be admitted to the state mental hospital. Neither the woman nor her husband was a Christian, but he consented to let her attend our services with her neighbor. Within a week the woman had been saved, healed, filled with the Holy Spirit, and she never did go to the mental hospital.

People can become sick mentally as well as physically, and God can heal mental illnesses as easily as He can physical illnesses. We must recognize that God has not given us a spirit of fear. We must learn to stand against the enemy.

Remember, confession of fear gives fear dominion over you. Your fears become stronger and you come more into the bondage of the enemy. But if you confess your Father's care, confess His protection, confess His Word, boldly confess that what God says about you is true, confess that greater is He that is in you than he that is in the world, you will rise above satanic influence every time.

When you confess your doubts and fears, your weakness and diseases, you are openly confessing that the Word of God is not true and that God has failed to make it good. His Word declares that by His stripes you were healed.

1 PETER 2:24
24 Who his own self bare our sins in his own body on the tree, that we, being dead to sins, should live unto righteousness: by whose stripes ye were healed.

MATTHEW 8:17
17 That it might be fulfilled which was spoken by Esaias the prophet, saying, Himself took our infirmities, and bare our sicknesses.

If instead of confessing that Jesus "took our infirmities, and bare our sicknesses," we declare that we still have them, we will remain sick. But when we start confessing that He already has done something about our sicknesses, we will receive healing.

Too often we accept the testimony of our physical senses instead of the testimony of God's Word. We must practice God's Word for it to work for us.

Memory Text:
"For God hath not given us the spirit of fear; but of power, and of love, and of a sound mind" (2 Tim. 1:7).

THE LESSON IN ACTION: *"But be ye doers of the word, and not hearers only . . ."* (James 1:22).

Faith for Prosperity

Bible Texts: Galatians 3:13,14,29; Deuteronomy 28:1-8,11,12

Central Truth: As born-again believers, we are redeemed from the curse of the law and are heirs to Abraham's blessing and God's promises of prosperity.

For many years I did not understand that it is God's will for His children to prosper. I thought, as many do, that poverty is a characteristic of humility — and in order to be humble, one must be poor.

I thought that a righteous man could not be wealthy, and a wealthy man could not be righteous.

I thought any promise in the Scriptures regarding financial blessing applied only to the Jews. I have since learned, through studying God's Word and applying it in my own life, that God wants His children to *"prosper and be in health, even as thy soul prospereth"* (3 John 2).

Someone might say, "The Bible says that money is the root of all evil." However, the Bible does not say that at all. First Timothy 6:10 says, *"For THE LOVE OF MONEY is the root of all evil: which while some coveted after, they have erred from the faith, and pierced themselves through with many sorrows."* A person can be guilty of that sin and not have one dime!

I have heard people say, "Well, I guess I'm just another Job." Some people think that poor old Job went through life poverty-stricken, sick, and afflicted. However, the entire Book of Job happened within a period of nine months, and the last chapter says God turned Job's captivity, and *"the Lord gave Job twice as much as he had before"* (Job 42:10).

When the thieves broke in and stole Job's things, he was in captivity to Satan. When the fire fell and burned up his crops, he was in captivity to Satan. When the storm came and blew the house down on his children and they were killed; when Job was smitten with boils from his head to his feet; when his wife turned against him and said, "Curse God and die," Job was in captivity to Satan. But God turned Job's captivity.

If you think you are another Job, that means you'll be one of the richest men around! You'll have twice as much as you've ever had before. You will be healed and live to be old. (Job lived 140 years after the events recorded in the Bible.) If you are another Job, you will prosper.

Redeemed from the Curse of the Law

GALATIANS 3:13,14,29
13 Christ hath redeemed us from the curse of the law, being made a curse for us: for

it is written, Cursed is every one that hangeth on a tree:

14 That the blessing of Abraham might come on the Gentiles through Jesus Christ; that we might receive the promise of the Spirit through faith....

29 And if ye be Christ's, then are ye Abraham's seed, and heirs according to the promise.

The above Scriptures tell us that Christ has redeemed us from the curse of the law. What, then, is the curse of the law? We turn for this answer to the first five books of the Old Testament, referred to as the Pentateuch, or the books of the Law. There we learn that the curse, or punishment, for breaking God's law is threefold: poverty, sickness, and the second death.

Christ has redeemed us from the curse of poverty. He has redeemed us from the curse of sickness. He has redeemed us from the curse of death — spiritual death now and physical death when Jesus comes again. We need have no fear of the second death.

Abraham's Blessing

Just as the curse is threefold in nature, so was Abraham's blessing. First, it was a material, financial blessing. Second, it was a physical blessing. Third, it was a spiritual blessing.

The New Testament Scripture Third John 2 agrees that God wants us to have material, physical, and spiritual prosperity, because it says, *"Beloved, I wish above all things that thou mayest prosper and be in health, even as thy soul prospereth."* Too

many people are under the impression that any promises in the Bible for material blessing and prosperity refer only to the Jews. However, this verse was written to New Testament Christians.

The word "Jew" is a short term or nickname for "Judah." The Israelites were never called Jews until after the split of the tribes. Judah didn't have any more promise of material and financial blessing than the other tribes of Israel. They received or inherited the blessing through their father Jacob. Jacob inherited the blessing through his father Isaac. Isaac inherited the blessing through his father Abraham. So it is not the Jews' blessing or promise. It is not Israel's blessing. *It is Abraham's blessing.* And that blessing is mine!

"That the blessing of Abraham might come on the Gentiles through Jesus Christ ..." (Gal. 3:14). In this third chapter of Galatians we also read, *"Know ye therefore that they which are of faith, the same are the children of Abraham"* (v. 7). If we are born-again Christians, *"then are ye Abraham's seed, and heirs according to the promise"* (Gal. 3:29).

After these Scriptures became plain to me and I saw what belonged to me as a child of God through faith in Him, other Scriptures began to open up to me. Everything belongs to God and is at His disposal.

"For every beast of the forest is mine, and the cattle upon a thousand hills ... for the world is mine, and the fulness thereof" (Ps. 50:10,12). *"The*

earth is the Lord's, and the fulness thereof..." (Ps. 24:1).

God created everything; then He made man, Adam, and gave him dominion over all of it. God made it all for His man Adam. He gave Adam dominion over the cattle on a thousand hills, over the silver and gold, over the world and the fullness thereof. In other words, Adam was the god of this world.

But Adam committed high treason and sold out to Satan. Thus, Satan became the god of this world. Jesus, however, came to redeem us from Satan's power and dominion over us. Romans 5:17 says, *"For if by one man's offence death reigned by one; much more they which receive abundance of grace and of the gift of righteousness shall reign in life by one, Jesus Christ."*

The Amplified version of this Scripture reads, "For if, because of one man's trespass (lapse, offense) death reigned through that one, much more surely will those who receive [God's] overflowing grace (unmerited favor) and the free gift of righteousness (putting them into right standing with Himself) reign as kings in life through the One, Jesus Christ, the Messiah, the Anointed One."

We are to reign as kings in life. That means that we have dominion over our lives. We are to dominate, not be dominated. Circumstances are not to dominate us. We are to dominate circumstances. Poverty is not to rule and reign over us. We are to rule and reign over poverty. Disease and sick-ness are not to rule and reign over us. We are to rule and reign over sickness. We are to reign as kings in life by Christ Jesus, in whom we have redemption.

DEUTERONOMY 28:1-8,11,12
1 And it shall come to pass, if thou shalt hearken diligently unto the voice of the Lord thy God, to observe and to do all his commandments which I command thee this day, that the Lord thy God will set thee on high above all nations of the earth:
2 And all these blessings shall come on thee, and overtake thee, if thou shalt hearken unto the voice of the Lord thy God.
3 Blessed shalt thou be in the city, and blessed shalt thou be in the field.
4 Blessed shall be the fruit of thy body, and the fruit of thy ground, and the fruit of thy cattle ...
5 Blessed shall be thy basket and thy store.
6 Blessed shalt thou be when thou comest in, and blessed shalt thou be when thou goest out.
7 The Lord shall cause thine enemies that rise up against thee to be smitten before thy face ...
8 The Lord shall command the blessing upon thee in thy storehouses, and in all that thou settest thine hand unto ...
11 And the Lord shall make thee plenteous in goods ...
12 The Lord shall open unto thee his good treasure, the heaven to give the rain unto thy land in his season, and to bless all the work of thine hand ...

The first part of Deuteronomy 28 lists the many ways the Lord would bless His people if they would obey Him. He promised to bless their children, their crops, and cattle. He promised to bless and protect them in battle. He promised to make them "plenteous in goods," and to bless them in "all that thou settest thine hand unto."

This blessing was all-inclusive, but it also was conditional. They must keep all of God's commandments. They must be a holy people, not straying from Him and seeking after other gods, but serving Him with all their hearts. The remainder of this chapter, verses 15 through 68, lists the curses that would fall upon His people if they did not keep His commandments.

When I first realized this truth and saw the prosperity, material and spiritual, that God has planned for His people, and that every born-again believer in Christ is an heir to this promise, I could hardly contain my joy!

I was thrilled to find out that I was redeemed from the curse of the law, from the curse of poverty, and that Abraham's blessing was mine.

We as Christians need not suffer financial setbacks; we need not be captive to poverty or sickness! God has provided healing and prosperity for His children if they will obey His commandments.

When Jesus was here on earth He said, *"If ye then, being evil, know how to give good gifts unto your children, HOW MUCH MORE shall your Father which is in heaven give good things to them that ask him?"* (Matt. 7:11).

How many of us who are parents want our children to go through life hungry, sick, or afflicted, never having enough to get along? No parent wants that. In fact, we work and sacrifice to try to help our children get a better education than we had so they can make a better living than we did.

God put all the cattle here; all the silver and gold. Is it reasonable to think that He did all of this only for the ungodly? Certainly He loves the sinner, but does He love the sinner more than His own children? No. God put all these things here for His people.

He said to Israel, *"If ye be willing and obedient, ye shall eat the good of the land"* (Isa. 1:19). And if God wants His children to eat the best, He wants them to wear the best clothing; He wants them to drive the best cars; He wants them to have the best of everything.

Proved Through Personal Experience

When this truth became real to my heart, the Lord spoke to me and said, "Don't pray for money anymore. You have authority through my Name to claim prosperity. I already have put gold, silver, and cattle on a thousand hills for my man Adam, and I gave him dominion over it. After he sold out to Satan, the second Adam, Jesus Christ, came to redeem you from the hand of the enemy and to remove you from the curse of the law. Now, instead of praying that I would do it, because I have made provision for your needs, all you need to do is say, 'Satan, take your hands off my money.' Just claim what you need. You reign in life by Christ Jesus."

At this time in my life, I was an evangelist. At the next church I went to I said, "Lord, if I get what I need here, this will have to work. The last time I was here I received only about $60 a week. I am going to claim $150 for this week." Then I said, "Satan, take your hands off my money in the Name of the Lord Jesus Christ."

You see, you never believe for the possible; you believe for the impossible. I was supposed to be in this church for just a week, but as it turned out, I was there ten days. I claimed $200 for these ten days. The pastor did not beg for money at all; he simply passed the offering plates, and when the offering was counted I had $240.

After that when I would go into churches to hold meetings, finances came in easily, and many times the pastor would say in amazement, "That is the biggest offering this church has ever given to an evangelist." And I had made no strong pleas at all. I had the key that unlocks the door.

Thank God, we are not under the curse, because Jesus has set us free! "For sickness I have health, for poverty wealth, since Jesus has ransomed me."

Memory Text:
"Beloved, I wish above all things that thou mayest prosper and be in health, even as thy soul prospereth" (3 John 2).

THE LESSON IN ACTION: *"But be ye doers of the word, and not hearers only ..."* (James 1:22).

58

Lesson 16

Seven Steps to the Highest Kind of Faith (Part 1)

Bible Texts: Colossians 1:12-14; 1 Corinthians 6:19,20

Central Truth: It is by the blood of the Lamb and the word of our testimony that we overcome Satan, we are delivered from the power of darkness, and we are translated into the kingdom of His dear Son.

I have a twofold purpose in mind in this series of lessons on faith. We already have covered most of these next points in some form or another, but I wanted to bring them together so you can check up on the progress you are making.

If you have studied these faith lessons and they have taken hold in your life, the devil is going to contest you. The Lord wants you to be prepared for the future, and through the power of God's Word you can be ready for any emergency that may arise.

Step 1 — The Integrity of the Word of God

The first thing you need to know is that the Word of God is actually what it declares itself to be. It is a revelation from God to us. It is God speaking to us *now*. Not only is it a book of the past and a book of the future; it also is a book of *now*. This book is a God-breathed, God-indwelt, and God-inspired message.

"For the word of God is quick, and powerful, and sharper than any twoedged sword, piercing even to the dividing asunder of soul and spirit, and of the joints and marrow, and is a discerner of the thoughts and intents of the heart" (Heb. 4:12). Moffatt's translation of this verse reads, "For the word of God is a living thing . . ." The word "quick" actually means "alive, living." The Word of God is a living thing. But it will only come alive to you as you accept it and act upon it.

So we see that the first step toward the highest kind of faith is to accept and understand the integrity of God's Word. The Word is of foremost importance.

Some people think God hasn't spoken to them unless they have a message in tongues or prophecy. But the Word of God *is* God speaking to us.

The gifts of prophecy, tongues, and interpretation of tongues do not supersede the Word. The Word comes first. These inspirational vocal gifts are given to us to inspire us in line with the Word, but if they say something apart from the Word, it is not the Holy Spirit speaking; that person is just speaking from his own thinking. You always must judge these things in the light of God's Word.

Also, there are those who try to read certain things into the Word because they want it to say what they believe. They are trying to fit the Word to their beliefs rather than fitting their beliefs to the Word.

Some people try to overlook certain passages or explain them away. But you must accept the Word for what it says and walk in the light of it. You must believe what the Word says, not what you *think* it says.

As you begin to study the Word in this light, accepting it as it is, you will be amazed to learn that some of the things you always have believed are not in the Word at all. You will wonder why you believed some things the way you did.

I found this true in my own experience. As I lay for many months on the bed of sickness, studying the Bible, I saw in it truths of faith and healing. These were new to me, because my church didn't teach about healing. But the more I studied God's Word, the more I saw it was true. And regardless of my church's teaching, I determined I was going to walk in the light of God's Word, because I believed that this Word is God speaking to us today. When I made this commitment, the biggest part of the battle was won.

To actually believe God's Word, I had to go against not only the teachings of my church but of my family as well. It is amazing how we can become more church-minded than Bible-minded. And sometimes our loved ones, thinking they have our best interests at heart, will oppose us from walking in the fullest light of God's Word. Nevertheless, I determined to follow the Word of God, knowing that this is God speaking to me today.

Step 2 — Our Redemption in Christ

The second thing you need to know is the reality of our redemption in Christ — not as a doctrine, philosophy, or creed of some kind — but an actual redemption from the authority of Satan. By the New Birth we have been translated into the kingdom of His Son, the Kingdom of God. In other words, we have been born into the very family of God.

COLOSSIANS 1:12-14
12 Giving thanks unto the Father, which hath made us meet [able] to be partakers of the inheritance of the saints in light:
13 Who hath delivered us from the power of darkness, and hath translated us into the kingdom of his dear Son:
14 In whom we have redemption through his blood, even the forgiveness of sins.

How wonderful that we *can* enter into our inheritance in Christ. God has made us *able* to have part of this inheritance, as we have just read.

Verse 13 goes on to say, *"Who hath delivered us from the power of darkness ..."* The Greek word translated "power" here means "authority." *"Who hath delivered us from the AUTHORITY of darkness ..."* refers to Satan's kingdom. Notice, too, that the Scripture doesn't say that He is going to deliver us. It says, *"Who HATH delivered us ..."*

Verse 14 tells us the price of redemption. *"In whom we have redemption through his blood..."* In connection with this Scripture let us look at Revelation 12:11, *"And they overcame him by the blood of the Lamb, and by the word of their testimony..." The American Revised Version* of this verse reads, "... because of the blood of the Lamb and because of the word of their testimony."

The blood of Jesus is the basis for our victory. But we have to add our testimony, our confession, to it. We have to stand our ground with the enemy.

Because Satan is the god of this world, he will try to have authority over you. But he needn't win, because you have been delivered through the blood of Jesus Christ from the power of darkness; from the authority of Satan. By virtue of the New Birth, you have been translated into the kingdom of His dear Son. In every contest with Satan you can overcome, no matter what the test may be, because you have redemption through the blood of the Lamb and because of the word of your testimony.

There Is Power in the Blood!

Satan's dominion over us as new creatures in Christ is ended. Jesus is the Lord and Head of this new Body.

He is referred to in the Scriptures as the Head of the Church. The Church, which is all born-again believers, is called the Body of Christ. Satan has no right to rule over the Body of Christ. Christ is the Head of the Body. He is the One who is to rule and dominate the Body.

Some people accept defeat in life because they don't fully understand the Word. They have told me that they didn't succeed because it wasn't God's will. They have said, "Our spirits belong to the Lord, but our bodies haven't been redeemed as yet. Therefore, we must suffer sickness and disease in the physical realm now. But the time is coming when we won't have to." In answer to this I turn to First Corinthians 6.

1 CORINTHIANS 6:19,20
19 What? know ye not that your body is the temple of the Holy Ghost which is in you, which ye have of God, and ye are not your own?
20 For ye are bought with a price: therefore glorify God in your body, and in your spirit, which are God's.

This passage tells us that not only our spirit, but also our body is bought with a price. Therefore you are to *"glorify God in your body and in your spirit, which are God's."* Does God get any glory out of Satan's dominating us physically? Could God get any glory out of the body, the temple of the Holy Spirit, which is deformed or defaced with sickness? Certainly not. We need to understand this clearly, and we need to learn to take a stand against the devil when he attacks our bodies — just as we would when he attacks our spirits.

Let us look again at Colossians 1:12, *"Giving thanks unto the Father, which hath made us meet* [able] *to be partakers of the inheritance of the saints in light."* This is part of our inheritance as children of God as we walk in the light. We have dominion and authority over the devil through the blood of Jesus. It is by the blood of the Lamb *and* the word of our testimony that we overcome Satan, we are delivered from the power of darkness, and we are translated into the kingdom of His dear Son.

Notice the words, *"Giving thanks unto the Father, which hath made us ABLE to be partakers of the inheritance ..."* We can partake of our inheritance right now. We don't have to relegate that to the future. We have an inheritance now. We have deliverance and redemption from the hand of Satan *now.* We can overcome him *now* by the blood of the Lamb and by the word of our testimony. We can glorify God *now* in our bodies and in our spirits, which are God's.

Memory Text:
"And they overcame him by the blood of the Lamb, and by the word of their testimony ..." (Rev. 12:11).

THE LESSON IN ACTION: *"But be ye doers of the word, and not hearers only ..."* (James 1:22).

Seven Steps to the Highest Kind of Faith (Part 2)

Bible Texts: 2 Corinthians 5:17; 1 John 1:3,4,7; John 14:13,14

Central Truth: Fellowship is the very mother of faith. It is the parent of joy. It is the source of victory.

As we press on in our study of God's Word toward a deeper understanding of the meaning of faith, let us examine three more steps to the highest kind of faith.

These steps will impress on us the reality of: (1) the new creation, (2) our fellowship with the Father, and (3) the authority of Jesus' Name.

Step 3 — The Reality of the New Creation

2 CORINTHIANS 5:17
17 Therefore if any man be in Christ, he is a new creature: old things are passed away; behold, all things are become new.

To achieve the highest kind of faith, it is necessary for us to know the reality of the new creation. We need to know that in the mind of God, we were created in Christ Jesus after He had been made sin as our Substitute.

We should know that the moment we accepted Christ as Savior and confessed Him as Lord, we were *recreated.* That is when the legal aspect became a reality in our life.

Today we have in our spirits the very life and nature of God. This is not an experience, it is not a religion, nor is it joining a church. It is an actual birth of our spirit.

We are the very sons and daughters of God. He is our very own Father. We know we have passed from Satan's dominion and spiritual death into the realm of life through Jesus Christ.

"We know that we have passed from death unto life, because we love the brethren ..." (1 John 3:14). We know we are in the family of God. We are children of God. One cannot join this family; he must be born into it.

How does this affect us in everyday life? If God is our very own Father and we are His very own children, we have as much freedom and fellowship with the Father as Jesus had in His earthly walk, because the Father loves us even as He loved Jesus! John 17:23 says, *"... that the world may know that thou hast sent me, and hast loved them, AS THOU HAST LOVED ME."*

Colossians 1:18 says, *"And he is the head of the body, the church: who is the beginning, the firstborn from the dead; that in all things he might have the preeminence."* Jesus is the firstborn, but we, too, are born again from the dead.

Peter said, *"Being born again, not*

of corruptible seed, but of incorruptible, by the word of God, which liveth and abideth for ever" (1 Peter 1:23).

We are begotten of God. We are born of God. We are God's children, heirs of God and joint (equal) heirs with Christ.

When we say this, we are not magnifying ourselves; we are magnifying God and what He has done for us through the Lord Jesus. We did not make ourselves new creatures; He made us new creatures. He is the Author and Finisher of our faith: *"For we are his workmanship, created in Christ Jesus unto good works ..."* (Eph. 2:10). We didn't make ourselves who and what we are; God did.

When a person belittles himself, he is actually belittling God's workmanship. He is criticizing something God has made. We should quit looking at ourselves from the natural standpoint, and instead see ourselves as God sees us, as created in Christ Jesus. The Father doesn't see us as anybody else sees us. He sees us in Christ.

Many Christians are defeated because they look at themselves from the natural standpoint. They could be victorious by looking at themselves as God does.

A Christian who was having severe problems in his life once said to me, "I guess I'm just paying for the life I lived before I got saved. I was so sinful." However, when we are born again, we are redeemed not only from sin, but from the penalty of sin. We do not have to pay for our sins; Christ already has done this for us. It is not even possible for us to pay for them.

Many people don't know the difference between repentance and doing penance. Yet if you would accuse them of following the teachings of certain other religions, they would hotly deny it. But that is exactly what they are doing — trying to do penance for their past life.

After a man repents, God no longer has any knowledge that that man ever did anything wrong! *"I, even I, am he that blotteth out thy transgressions for mine own sake, and WILL NOT REMEMBER THY SINS"* (Isa. 43:25). If God doesn't remember, why should you?

If after being saved, a man had to continue to reap what he had sown as a sinner, he would then have to go to hell when he died, because that's part of the penalty, too. If he is going to reap any part of the penalty, he will reap all of it. But we are redeemed not only from the power, but also from the penalty of sin. Jesus took our place. He suffered the penalty for our sin. He has made us able to enjoy the inheritance of saints in light, as we discussed in our last lesson.

Step 4 — The Reality of Our Fellowship With the Father

The very heart reason for redemption is fellowship. *"God is faithful, by whom ye were called unto the fellowship of his Son Jesus Christ our Lord"* (1 Cor. 1:9). Notice here that we were called *"unto the fellowship of his Son."*

1 JOHN 1:3,4,7

3 That which we have seen and heard declare we unto you, that ye also may have fellowship with us: and truly our fellowship is with the Father, and with his Son Jesus Christ.

4 And these things write we unto you, that your joy may be full . . .

7 But if we walk in the light, as he is in the light, we have fellowship one with another, and the blood of Jesus Christ his Son cleanseth us from all sin.

The highest honor the Father has conferred upon us is that of having joint fellowship with Him, with His Son, and with the Holy Spirit in carrying out His dream for the redemption of the human race.

Relationship without fellowship is an insipid thing. It is like marriage without love or companionship.

Fellowship is the very mother of faith. It is the parent of joy. It is the source of victory. And He has called us individually into fellowship with His Son.

If we have fellowship with Him and we are walking in the light as He is in the light, then prayer becomes one of the sweetest and greatest privileges we have.

To hear some people talk, one would think prayer is pure drudgery. We hear them talk about fighting and struggling; about trying to believe. But it never has been a problem or a fight for me to pray. It always has been a joy. It never has taken anything out of me to pray; it puts something in me. I often pray five or more hours a day.

The trouble with people who have

such difficulty with prayer is that instead of letting the Holy Spirit help them and pray through them, they try to do it all on their own — in their own energy. Naturally this wears them out. God wants us to come to the place of resting in Him: *"For with stammering lips and another tongue will he speak to this people. To whom he said, This is the rest wherewith ye may cause the weary to rest; and this is the refreshing . . ."* (Isa. 28:11,12). We can find a time of refreshing in the Lord as we pray in other tongues.

Step 5 — The Reality of the Authority of Jesus' Name

JOHN 14:13,14

13 And whatsoever ye shall ask in my name, that will I do, that the Father may be glorified in the Son.

14 If ye shall ask any thing in my name, I will do it.

Suppose a wealthy man were to give you a signed statement stating that you were entitled to use his name and thereby receive anything you might need in order to live comfortably.

Suppose this was a legal document, given before witnesses, whereby every one of your needs could be met for the rest of your life. Does this sound too good to be true? The wonderful part of it is that it *is* true!

God has given us "the power of attorney" to use the Name of Jesus to meet our every need: spiritual, physical, or financial. He has given us power over satanic forces. He has said

He would give us "whatsoever ye shall ask in my name."

We have that authority to use His Name. The fact that many do not is not a matter of lack of faith, but a matter of not knowing our legal rights in Christ. It is a matter of taking the place of a son or daughter and taking advantage of our rights as a child of God. It is a matter of knowing what belongs to us and doing what the Word says.

Memory Text:
"God is faithful, by whom ye were called unto the fellowship of his Son Jesus Christ our Lord" (1 Cor. 1:9).

THE LESSON IN ACTION: *"But be ye doers of the word, and not hearers only ..."* (James 1:22).

Lesson 18

Seven Steps to the Highest Kind of Faith (Part 3)

Bible Texts: 2 Corinthians 6:14-16; Romans 3:23-26; Psalm 32:1,2

Central Truth: We can approach God with full assurance, because we have been made the righteousness of God in Christ Jesus.

This lesson brings us to Step 6 in our study of the highest faith. In it we want to help you gain new insight into the meaning of the words "righteous" and "righteousness," as shown in the Scriptures.

Step 6 — The Reality of Our Righteousness

2 CORINTHIANS 6:14-16

14 Be ye not unequally yoked together with unbelievers: for what fellowship hath righteousness with unrighteousness? and what communion hath light with darkness?
15 And what concord hath Christ with Belial? or what part hath he that believeth with an infidel?
16 And what agreement hath the temple of God with idols? for ye are the temple of the living God; as God hath said, I will dwell in them, and walk in them; and I will be their God, and they shall be my people.

Many people see in the above passage only a teaching about separation from the world, and they immediately practice *segregation*, thinking it is *separation*. They feel they cannot have anything to do with the world or anyone in the world. They even segregate themselves from other Christians if they don't completely agree with them.

However, Jesus said, *"Ye are the salt of the earth... Ye are the light of the world..."* (Matt. 5:13,14). In order to be the salt and light in the world, we must remain *in* the world, doing our job for the Lord.

A man once said to me, "I am the only Christian where I work. Pray that God will move me out."

"Oh, no," I told him. "The place would really be corrupt without your influence. You stay right there. You're the salt of the earth; you stay right there and salt it." We are *in* the world, but we are not *of* the world.

Notice something equally important about this passage: Believers are called "believers," and unbelievers are called "unbelievers." Believers are called "righteousness," and unbelievers are referred to as "unrighteousness." Believers are called "light" and unbelievers "darkness."

The idea of calling yourself "righteousness" sounds egotistical, yet people do not object to calling themselves "believers," or "light." This passage uses all three terms to refer to believers!

In verse 15 we see the Church, or believers, referred to as Christ, because He is the Head and we are the

Body. And, of course, our head doesn't go by one name and our body by another. The Church is Christ, and we are the Body of Christ.

ROMANS 3:23-26

23 For all have sinned, and come short of the glory of God;

24 Being justified freely by his grace through the redemption that is in Christ Jesus:

25 Whom God hath set forth to be a propitiation through faith in his blood, to declare his righteousness for the remission of sins that are past, through the forbearance of God;

26 To declare, I say, at this time his righteousness: that he might be just, and the justifier of him which believeth in Jesus.

In this passage, the Greek word that can be translated "righteousness" or "righteous" is translated "just" and "justifier." In other words, verse 26 could just as easily read, "that he might be *righteous,* and the *righteousness* of him which believeth in Jesus."

What does all this mean? What is God teaching us through this Scripture? That God through Jesus declared His righteousness. That God Himself is righteous, and that God is my righteousness. He is the "righteousness of him which believeth in Jesus."

Romans 5:17 says, *"For if by one man's offence death reigned by one; much more they which receive abundance of grace and of the gift of righteousness shall reign in life by one, Jesus Christ."*

Most people have thought that righteousness is something a person attains by right living. Righteousness does mean rightness or right standing, but this Scripture says it is a *gift* — not something we can earn by good deeds and clean living.

A *gift* is something we receive instantly; a stage of spiritual development is *fruit.* If righteousness were fruit, the Scripture would read, "and the fruit of righteousness." However, it says, "the *gift* of righteousness."

Every one of God's dear children has the same righteousness and standing with God. He doesn't love one person more than another. He doesn't listen to one person's prayers more than another's. When this truth fully sinks in, your prayers will work! Your prayers will get answered!

Many people struggle along in the realm of self-condemnation, allowing the enemy to rob them of the inheritance that is theirs in Christ Jesus. They think their prayers won't work and God won't hear them. They think if they could just find a righteous man to pray for them, his prayers would work.

How sad they have not seen the truths in the Scriptures we just read. God is our righteousness. He became our righteousness when He imparted His nature, eternal life, to us when we were born again. He became our righteousness the moment we accepted Jesus as our Savior and confessed Him as our Lord.

I first discovered the truths of these Scriptures as I lay bedfast for 16 months as a teenager. I did not understand these Scriptures then. At first they were a small gleam of light in a dark corner. I was having the same struggles many of you have to overcome problems in your life or health.

Reading my Bible, one day I came across James 5:14,15: *"Is any sick among you? let him call for the elders of the church; and let them pray over him, anointing him with oil in the name of the Lord: And the prayer of faith shall save the sick, and the Lord shall raise him up; and if he have committed any sins, they shall be forgiven him."*

As I read, any faith that momentarily flickered in my heart was quickly extinguished by the thought that my church didn't believe in healing or anointing with oil.

Then the Lord spoke to me and said, "It is *the prayer of faith* that heals the sick. You can pray that prayer yourself as well as anybody can."

I was just a babe in Christ. I was 16 years old and had been saved only a few months, yet the Lord said I could pray that prayer! But immediately my wrong thinking defeated me. I thought, *Yes, I could — if I were righteous.* (I was acquainted with all my shortcomings, and I knew I wasn't righteous; at least not according to my understanding of the word.)

Reading further in James, I read where Elijah is an example of a righteous man praying: *"Elias was a man subject to like passions as we are, and he prayed earnestly that it might not rain: and it rained not on the earth by the space of three years and six months"* (James 5:17).

As I studied about Elijah, I decided he was not my idea of a righteous man. When the hand of the Lord was upon him, he could outrun the king's chariot. But when he learned that Queen Jezebel wanted to kill him, he ran and hid under a juniper tree, begging the Lord to let him die. Then he whined to the Lord, "Everybody has backslidden but me. I'm the only one who is serving You, Lord."

Such inconsistency is hardly the mark of a righteous man. I wondered, *How could James have given him as an example of a righteous men praying? He was no more righteous than I!*

Then I remembered James said Elijah was *"a man subject to like passions as we are."* Not only was he subject to these passions; he also gave in to them. Even though he allowed discouragement to dominate his actions, he was called a righteous man.

A Better Covenant

PSALM 32:1,2
1 Blessed is he whose transgression is forgiven, whose sin is covered.
2 Blessed is the man unto whom the Lord imputeth not iniquity, and in whose spirit there is no guile.

Under the Old Covenant, the blood of innocent animals covered sin. God did not impute iniquity to people, even though they had sinned. He covered their sin, forgave it, and imputed righteousness to them. In His sight, they were righteous. "... *When I see the blood, I will pass over you,*" He said in Exodus 12:13.

If God did this for His children under the law, how much more will He do for us? Under grace we have a better covenant, established upon better promises. The blood of Jesus Christ not only covers our sins; it cleanses us "from all unrighteousness." Revelation 1:5 says, "... *Unto him that loved us, and washed us from our sins in his own blood.*"

As I read this Scripture, I saw that when I had been born again, all my sins were remitted, and my past life ceased. I saw that I had become a new creature in Christ, and I knew He didn't make any unrighteous new creatures.

Immediately the devil was right there, saying, "That may be true, but what about since then? It wasn't very long ago that you lost your temper. That's certainly no way for a righteous person to act." He got me looking at the natural again instead of at God's Word.

Then I read First John 1:9, "*If we confess our sins, he is faithful and just to forgive us our sins, and to cleanse us from all unrighteousness.*" (This Scripture wasn't written to sinners, but to believers.)

This meant I became the righteousness of God in Christ when I was born again. If I had sinned since that time — and I had — I just confessed my sins and He forgave me and cleansed me from my unrighteousness. (If I'm cleansed from unrighteousness, then I'm righteous again.)

Before this, when I had read James 5:16 — "*... The effectual fervent prayer of a righteous man availeth much*" — I had thought if I could ever become righteous, I would have a tremendous prayer life and see outstanding answers to prayer.

Now I saw that my prayers would work, because God would hear me as quickly as He would anybody else. In my Bible, beside James 5:16, I wrote the words, "I am that Righteous Man."

This is not bragging on anything I have done; it is bragging on what I am in Christ. It is praising God for what He has wrought for us in Christ.

This means we can stand in God's presence without any sense of guilt, condemnation, or inferiority. This means the prayer problem is settled. No longer do we need to go into God's presence tongue-tied because of condemnation, or filled with fear because of ignorance.

We can enter His presence in full assurance because we have been made righteous through the blood of our Lord Jesus Christ.

Memory Text:
"*For he hath made him to be sin for us, who knew no sin; that we might be made the righteousness of God in him*" (2 Cor. 5:21).

THE LESSON IN ACTION: "*But be ye doers of the word, and not hearers only ...*" (James 1:22).

Lesson 19

Seven Steps to the Highest Kind of Faith (Part 4)

Bible Texts: 1 Corinthians 6:19,20; 2 Corinthians 6:16; Acts 8:14,15; 9:17; 19:1,2

Central Truth: God Himself, in the person of the Holy Spirit, dwells within the believer.

Too often those who have been filled with the Holy Spirit think they have received simply a wonderful blessing, or some kind of rich spiritual experience. They miss the teaching of the Word entirely. First John 4:4 says, *"... greater is he that is in you, than he that is in the world."*

The infilling of the Holy Spirit means that He — the Holy Spirit — comes to dwell in us. Jesus said, *"And I will pray the Father, and he shall give you another Comforter, that HE MAY ABIDE WITH YOU FOR EVER"* (John 14:16).

Therefore, the seventh — and an extremely vital — step in our search for the highest kind of faith is to realize that our body is the temple of God. *God Himself, in the person of the Holy Spirit, dwells within us!*

Step 7 — The Reality of the Indwelling Spirit

In Old Testament times, God's earthly dwelling place was the tabernacle, or Temple. But since Christ died on the cross, rose again, and returned to heaven, sending the Holy Spirit upon the believers on the Day of Pentecost, He no longer dwells in a man-made Holy of Holies. Our bodies have become His temple!

1 CORINTHIANS 6:19,20
19 What? know ye not that your body is the temple of the Holy Ghost which is in you, which ye have of God, and ye are not your own?
20 For ye are bought with a price: therefore glorify God in your body, and in your spirit, which are God's.
2 CORINTHIANS 6:16
16 ... for ye are the temple of the living God; as God hath said, I will dwell in them, and walk in them; and I will be their God, and they shall be my people.

In every crisis of life, we should instinctively say, "I am a conqueror. I am more than a victor, for the Creator dwells in me. The Greater One lives in me. He can put me over. He can make me a success. I cannot fail!" This is not bragging on yourself. It is bragging on the One who is in you.

Too often, however, Spirit-filled believers cringe before the trials of life, and needlessly allow the devil to defeat them. They run around crying on one another's shoulders, praying pitiful, weak little prayers, wondering why victory doesn't come. Yet all the time

71

help is present — because the Holy Spirit is inside them ready to help them!

The Enduement of Power on the Early Church

In the New Testament Church, it was the *exception* rather than the rule to have any believers who had *not* received the infilling of the Holy Spirit with the supernatural sign of speaking in other tongues. The apostles recognized the necessity of the indwelling Spirit of God, and they stressed this in their teachings to new converts.

ACTS 8:14,15
14 Now when the apostles which were at Jerusalem heard that Samaria had received the word of God, they sent unto them Peter and John:
15 Who, when they were come down, prayed for them, that they might receive the Holy Ghost.

ACTS 9:17
17 And Ananias went his way, and entered into the house; and putting his hands on him said, Brother Saul, the Lord, even Jesus, that appeared unto thee in the way as thou camest, hath sent me, that thou mightest receive thy sight, and be filled with the Holy Ghost.

ACTS 19:1,2
1 And it came to pass, that, while Apollos was at Corinth, Paul having passed through the upper coasts came to Ephesus: and finding certain disciples,
2 He said unto them, Have ye received the Holy Ghost since ye believed? And they said unto him, We have not so much as heard whether there be any Holy Ghost.

Certainly the Church today is no less in need of this enduement of power!

The Apostle Paul said, *"Know ye not that ye are the temple of God, and that the Spirit of God dwelleth in you?"* (1 Cor. 3:16).

The Amplified version of this verse reads, "Do you not discern and understand that you [the whole church at Corinth] are God's temple (His sanctuary), and that God's Spirit has His permanent dwelling in you — to be at home in you [collectively as a church and also individually]?"

We are the temple of God. God indwells us not only as a Body, but as individuals.

Notice the expression, "to be at home in you." God is actually making His home in our bodies! No longer does He dwell in a man-made Holy of Holies, as in Old Testament times.

In those times, it was required that every Jewish male present himself before the Lord at least once a year in Jerusalem. The men had to travel to Jerusalem, because the presence of God was *only* in the Holy of Holies. No one except the High Priest dared approach the holy presence, and he only with great precautions. Anyone else who intruded into the holy place fell dead instantly.

But now all this has been done away with, and we may *"... come boldly unto the throne of grace, that we may obtain mercy, and find grace to help in time of need"* (Heb. 4:16).

Just before Jesus died, He said, *"It is finished."* He was not talking about the Plan of Redemption's being finished, because it wasn't finished when He died. He had to rise from the dead and ascend into the heavenly Holy of Holies with His own blood as a sacrifice to obtain eternal redemption for us.

Then He had to ascend on high to be seated at the right hand of the Father and begin His mediatorial intercession; to be the Mediator between God and man. Until then, the New Covenant was not in effect.

No, when Jesus said on the cross, *"It is finished,"* He was referring to the Old Testament's being finished!

When this happened, the veil, or curtain, that separated the Holy of Holies was torn in two from top to bottom.

The Jewish historian Josephus tells us this curtain was 40 feet wide, 20 feet high, and 4 inches thick. Imagine how difficult it would be for a man to tear something this size in two! But notice that the Scriptures do not say the curtain was torn from the bottom to the top. Rather, *"... the veil of the temple was rent in twain from the TOP TO THE BOTTOM ..."* (Matt. 27:51). This signified that it was God, not man, who tore down the curtain — the barrier — separating man from God!

The presence of God moved out of that man-made Holy of Holies never to dwell there again. Now His divine presence indwells us.

To be filled with the Holy Spirit is much more than just a thrilling experience. The Holy Spirit, the divine personality, actually comes to live in you!

"... For ye are the temple of the living God; as God hath said, I WILL DWELL IN THEM, AND WALK IN THEM; and I will be their God, and they shall be my people" (2 Cor. 6:16).

How many of us fully realize this marvelous truth? How many of us recognize the fact that in us — ready for our use — is *all the power we will ever need to put us over in life?*

If we will begin to believe what the Bible says — to confess what God's Word says — the Holy Spirit will rise up within us and give illumination to our minds. He will give direction to our spirits, health to our bodies, and help in every aspect of life. We can be conscious of His indwelling presence every moment.

Let us look again at *The Amplified* version of First Corinthians 3:16, "... God's Spirit has His permanent dwelling in you — to be at home in you ..."

Few of us are conscious of God's living in our bodies, for we could not be conscious of His living within us and still talk the way we do!

For example, when asked to do some difficult thing, how quick we are to say, "No, I can't do that."

Why do we do this? It is because we are trusting in ourselves to do it, and we know we don't have the ability. But if we know He is in us, we know He has the ability. We change the "I can't" to "I can," because we are trusting in Him.

We say, "I can, because He is in me. Greater is He that is in me than he that is in the world." No matter what impossibilities we may be facing, we can say, "He will make me a success, because He indwells me."

This kind of believing — this kind of talking — is faith talking, and it will put Him to work for us.

Some people have a wrong conception of the Holy Spirit's role in their lives. They think He will come in, take over, and run the show. They expect Him to become sort of a boss, without their having to do anything.

The Holy Spirit, however, is a gentleman. He will guide and direct us; He will prompt and urge; but He never will force or control our life.

Demons and evil spirits *control* those whom they enter, forcing them to do things they don't want to do, but the Holy Spirit gently leads and guides us. He won't do anything until we put Him to work for us, because He is sent to be our Helper. He is not sent to *do* the job, but to *help* us do it.

The Amplified version of Ephesians 3:16,17 says, "May he grant you out of the rich treasury of His glory to be strengthened and reinforced with mighty power in the inner man by the (Holy) Spirit [Himself] — indwelling your innermost being and personality. May Christ through your faith [actually] dwell — settle down, abide, make His permanent home — in your hearts! May you be rooted deep in love and founded securely on love."

In this passage of Scripture, Paul was writing to those who already were born again and filled with the Holy Spirit.

How does Christ abide in our hearts? Through our faith. Christ wants to dwell in our hearts; to reign as King on the throne of our hearts. But too few have allowed Him to do so.

People look outside themselves for God to do something. They sing, "Come by here, Lord. Come by here." (We think if we could only get Him to "come by here," He might do something for us!)

Then we sing, "Reach out and touch the Lord as He goes by." But this is all sense knowledge. It is all on the outside. It is all physical.

Someone might argue, "But in the Bible didn't the woman with the issue of blood reach out and touch the Lord?" Yes, but that was when He was here on the earth in physical form. Now He is not only *with* us; He is *in* us. We don't have to reach out and touch Him; He is always in us.

But this is not going to do us any good unless we know it and believe it, because the Holy Spirit will not rise up and take over. When we know He is in there, and we act intelligently on God's Word, He will work through us.

We can say, "Greater is He that is in me than he that is in the world. The Greater One is in me. I am depending on Him. He will put me over. He will make me a success, because He is in me. The Master of Creation is making His home in my body."

Memory Text:
". . . *Greater is he that is in you, than he that is in the world*" (1 John 4:4).

THE LESSON IN ACTION: *"But be ye doers of the word, and not hearers only . . ."* (James 1:22).

Lesson 20

Six Enemies to Faith

Bible Texts: 2 Corinthians 5:17,21; John 16:23,24; Romans 10:10; Mark 11:23,24

Central Truth: When we "fight the good fight of faith," we can step out of the narrow place of failure into the boundless power of God.

Our lesson today discusses the Christian's "good fight of faith," as mentioned in First Timothy 6:12.

I have heard people say they were going to fight the devil. I don't know why, because, in the first place, they were no match for him. Second, Jesus already has defeated the devil for us. Jesus was our Substitute.

I also have heard people say they were going to fight sin. But I am not going to fight sin; I'm going to preach the *cure* for sin. Jesus is the cure for sin.

The only fight the believer is called upon to fight is "the good fight of faith." If there is such a fight, that implies there must be enemies or hindrances to faith (for if there were no enemies to faith, there would be no fight to it). In this lesson we will deal with six enemies to faith.

Enemy No. 1 — Failure To Understand What It Means To Be a New Creature in Christ

2 CORINTHIANS 5:17

17 Therefore if any man be in Christ, he is a new creature: old things are passed away; behold, all things are become new.

A lack of understanding of what it means to be a new creature hinders our faith life. Many people do not realize that they actually *are* new creatures. They think that when they were saved, God simply forgave them of their sins.

It would do little good if this were all the sinner received, for he is a child of the devil and still would go to hell. He has to be born again. He has to become a new creature, putting off his old, sinful ways.

No, we are not *just* forgiven sinners. We are not barely-getting-along church members. We are not living at the end of the block on Struggling-To-Get-to-Heaven Street next to Grumble Alley. That's not for us!

We are new creatures, created by God in Christ Jesus with the very life and nature of God in our spirits. We are children of God, sons of God, heirs of God, and joint-heirs with Christ Jesus.

Enemy No. 2 — Failure To Understand Our Place

Everywhere I go, I suggest that Christians go through the New Testament — particularly the epistles — and write down the phrases "in Christ," "in whom," and "in Him." Writing them down will help you remember them.

There are approximately 140 such expressions in the New Testament. If you will read and meditate on these Scriptures until they become a part of you, life will be different for you.

As you read these verses, say to yourself, "This is who I am. This is what I have in Christ Jesus."

In one church I visited, there was a woman whom the pastor described as one of the most outstanding Christian workers he had ever known. She had a degree in Christian education from a leading seminary, and she gave her time to the church free of charge.

During our revival there, I urged the people to begin memorizing and claiming these verses. After a while, this woman came to me and said she had been confessing 25 of these Scriptures, and she had become an entirely different person. She said she didn't worry any more. She said she thought and acted differently. She felt differently. She was amazed at herself.

I told her she was only then beginning to walk in the light of what she had had all the time. Like many Christians, she didn't have an understanding of what Christ was in her life. This hindered her faith. Getting this understanding cured her of her worry habit.

Enemy No. 3 — Failure To Understand Righteousness

2 CORINTHIANS 5:21
21 For he hath made him to be sin for us,

who knew no sin; that we might be made the righteousness of God in him.

The blood of Jesus cleanses us from all sin (1 John 1:7). Therefore, by the New Birth, we become a righteous new creature. We know God did not make any unrighteous new creatures. We are created by God in Christ Jesus, and He made us righteous new creatures.

We are sons and daughters of God as though we never had sinned. We can stand in His presence without sin-consciousness; without any feelings of guilt or shame. We don't have to be paralyzed with fear. We can come into God's presence because we belong there.

When we were born again, our sins were remitted, because our past life stopped existing. God said He wouldn't remember our transgressions (Jer. 31:34). And if *He* doesn't remember them, why should *we?*

Some might ask, "But I have committed sins since becoming a Christian. How can I be righteous?"

The answer to this question is found in First John 1:9, *"If we confess our sins, he is faithful and just to forgive us our sins, and to cleanse us from all unrighteousness."*

When the believer who has sinned confesses his sin and asks for forgiveness, the Lord does two things: (1) He forgives him; (2) He cleanses him from all unrighteousness.

When we sin, we feel guilty and have a sense of unrighteousness. We feel unworthy to come into God's presence. But when we confess our sins, He forgives and cleanses us. We regain our right standing with Him.

The word "unrighteousness" is simply the word "righteousness" with the prefix "un" in front of it; it means "not righteousness" or "non-righteousness." If we are cleansed from "non-righteousness," we are righteous again.

Enemy No. 4 — Failure To Understand Our Right To Use the Name of Jesus

JOHN 16:23,24

23 ... whatsoever ye shall ask the Father in my name, he will give it you.
24 Hitherto have ye asked nothing in my name: ask, and ye shall receive, that your joy may be full.

When we fully realize the power of Jesus' Name — when we understand what that Name will do — then we can defeat Satan and enjoy victory.

In the 16th chapter of Mark, Jesus told His disciples, *"Go ye into all the world, and preach the gospel to every creature. He that believeth and is baptized shall be saved; but he that believeth not shall be damned. And these signs shall follow them that believe ..."* (Mark 16:15-17).

These signs shall follow *those who believe* the Gospel — not just the Early Church, not just the apostles, not just the preachers. All believers can cast out devils in His Name. All believers have authority over evil spirits in the Name of Jesus. In His Name they will speak with new tongues. In His Name they will lay hands on the sick and they shall recover.

The Name of Jesus has authority and power today, and that Name belongs to us!

Enemy No. 5 — Failure To Act Upon the Word

If we know that God's Word is true, and we act as if it is true, it becomes a reality in our lives.

The Bible says, *"Trust in the Lord with all thine heart; and lean not unto thine own understanding"* (Prov. 3:5). All that is necessary for us to ask is, "What does God's Word say?"

People often ask me why they don't receive healing. They quote such Scriptures as *"Himself took our infirmities, and bare our sicknesses"* (Matt. 8:17), and *"Who his own self bare our sins in his own body on the tree, that we, being dead to sins, should live unto righteousness: by whose stripes ye were healed"* (1 Peter 2:24).

They tell me they believe these Scriptures.

Then I ask them, "But have you ever *acted* like these Scriptures are true?"

When he was in his forties, A. B. Simpson, a Presbyterian minister who later founded the Christian and Missionary Alliance, was told he was dying of a heart condition and had only a few months to live.

He took a vacation to Old Orchard Beach, Maine, where he could spend time studying the Word of God on the subject of divine healing, a subject that had gained his interest. He writes in *The Gospel of Healing,* "... the summer I speak of I heard a great number of people testify that they had been healed by simply trusting the Word of Christ, just as they would for their salvation. It drove me to my Bible. I determined that I must settle this matter one way or the other.

"I am so glad I did not go to man," he continued. "At His feet, alone, with my Bible open, and with no one to help or guide me, I became convinced that this was part of Christ's glorious gospel for a sinful and suffering world, and the purchase of His blessed Cross, for all who would believe and receive His Word."

Simpson solemnly vowed to God that he accepted healing without question; that he took Jesus as his Healer; and that he would preach and minister healing in any way God asked him to.

Two days later, Simpson was invited to speak at a service in New Hampshire. He testified about Jesus and His faithfulness to heal and shared that he had just taken Jesus as his Healer.

The next day he was invited to go mountain climbing. His first reaction was that he couldn't go because of his heart condition. Then he remembered he had declared his healing, so he accepted the invitation. Until this time, he had not felt his healing; he had just declared it.

He battled all the way up the mountain. Every time he got his mind off the Scriptures, he felt weakness, pain, and fear. But as he overcame these feelings and claimed his healing, the symptoms would leave. He fought this battle all the way to the top of the mountain — and walked away victorious.

He went on to lead an active, energetic life in God's service, and he suffered no more symptoms. "I needed to step out and claim my victory," he concluded.

Real faith is the child of the knowledge of God's Word. Simpson acted on the Word and got real faith from it. Instead of *trying* to believe, he *acted* upon the Word.

Enemy No. 6 — Failure To Hold Fast to Our Confession of Faith

ROMANS 10:10
10 For with the heart man believeth unto righteousness; and with the mouth confession is made unto salvation.

MARK 11:23,24
23 For verily I say unto you, That whosoever shall say unto this mountain, Be thou removed, and be thou cast into the sea; and shall not doubt in his heart, but shall believe that those things which he saith shall come to pass; he shall have whatsoever he saith.
24 Therefore I say unto you, What things soever ye desire, when you pray, believe that ye receive them, and ye shall have them.

A young minister in St. Louis once said to me, "I am 32. Doctors have said it is impossible for my wife to have children. Will you talk and pray with us?"

As we talked and prayed together,

78

his wife said she would confess that they would have a child. In the past she had always said she would *like* to have a child. Now she would say that they *would* have a child.

Twelve months later I received a letter announcing that they had had a bouncing baby girl. All they needed was to act upon the Word.

Faith is measured by our confession. Our usefulness in the Lord is measured by our confession.

Eventually we become what we confess, whether for good or bad.

There is a confession of our hearts and a confession of our lips, and when these two harmonize, we become mighty in our prayer life.

The reason so many Christians are defeated is because they have a negative confession. They always are talking about their weaknesses and failures, and invariably they sink to the level of their confession.

There is a scriptural law I dis-covered from the lips of Jesus in Mark 11:23,24, which is quoted above. This is the law that *our confessions rule us. We are what we say.*

The woman with the issue of blood, whose story we find in Mark 5:25-34, said, *"If I may touch but his clothes, I shall be whole."* Jesus said, *"Daughter, thy faith hath made thee whole; go in peace, and be whole of thy plague."* What she said was her faith speaking — and it came to pass.

When we fight "the good fight of faith," as the Apostle Paul admonishes us, we can step out of the narrow place of failure and weakness in which we live into the boundless power of God.

Memory Text:
"Fight the good fight of faith, lay hold on eternal life, whereunto thou art also called, and hast professed a good profession before many witnesses" (1 Tim. 6:12).

THE LESSON IN ACTION: *"But be ye doers of the word, and not hearers only ..."* (James 1:22).

The God-Kind of Faith

Bible Texts: Mark 11:12-14,20-24; Romans 10:13,14,17

Central Truth: The kind of faith that spoke the universe into existence is dealt to our hearts.

There are two things to notice about the God-kind of faith. First, a man believes with his heart. Second, he believes with his words. It isn't enough just to believe in your heart. In order to get God to work for you, you must believe with your words also.

Jesus said, *"Whosoever shall say. . .and shall not doubt in his heart, but shall believe that those things which he saith shall come to pass; he shall have whatsoever he saith"* (Mark 11:23). This is the unalterable law of faith.

MARK 11:12-14,20-24

12 And on the morrow, when they were come from Bethany, he was hungry:

13 And seeing a fig tree afar off having leaves, he came, if haply he might find anything thereon: and when he came to it, he found nothing but leaves; for the time of figs was not yet.

14 And Jesus answered and said unto it, No man eat fruit of thee hereafter for ever. And his disciples heard it. . . .

20 And in the morning, as they passed by, they saw the fig tree dried up from the roots.

21 And Peter calling to remembrance saith unto him, Master, behold, the fig tree which thou cursedst is withered away.

22 And Jesus answering saith unto them, Have faith in God.

23 For verily I say unto you, That whosoever shall say unto this mountain, Be thou removed, and be thou cast into the sea; and shall not doubt in his heart, but shall believe that those things which he saith shall come to pass; he shall have whatsoever he saith.

24 Therefore I say unto you, What things soever ye desire, when ye pray, believe that ye receive them, and ye shall have them.

Let us focus our attention on the statement "Have faith in God," or, as the margin reads, "Have the faith of God." Greek scholars tell us this should be translated, "Have the God-kind of faith."

Jesus demonstrated that He had the God-kind of faith. While He was afar off, He saw that the fig tree had leaves. But as He approached it, looking for fruit, He saw it was barren. Some have questioned why Jesus looked for figs on this tree when it was not the season for the figs to be ripe. However, in that country, trees that retained their leaves usually also had figs.

Finding no fruit on the tree, Jesus said, *"No man eat fruit of thee hereafter for ever."*

The next day as Jesus and His disciples passed by again, they found the tree dried up from its roots. Amazed, Peter said, *"Master, behold,* the fig tree which thou cursedst is withered away."

It was then that Jesus made the statement, "Have faith in God [have the faith of God, or the God-kind of faith]. For verily I say unto you, That whosoever shall say unto this mountain, Be thou removed, and be thou cast into the sea; and shall not doubt in his heart, but shall believe that those things which he saith shall come to pass; he shall have whatsoever he saith" (vv. 22,23).

After telling His disciples in verse 22 to have the God-kind of faith, Jesus went on to explain what this meant: The God-kind of faith is the kind of faith in which a man believes with his heart and says with his mouth that which he believes in his heart — and it comes to pass.

Jesus showed He had that kind of faith, because He believed what He said would come to pass. He said to the tree, "No man eat fruit of thee hereafter for ever."

This is the kind of faith that spoke the world into existence! "Through faith we understand that the worlds were framed by the word of God, so that things which are seen were not made of things which do appear" (Heb. 11:3).

How did He do it? God believed that what He said would come to pass. He spoke the Word, and there was an earth. He spoke the vegetable kingdom into existence. He spoke the animal kingdom into existence. He spoke the heavens, the moon, the sun, the stars, and the universe into existence. He said it, and it was so!

That is the God-kind of faith. God believed what He said would come to pass, and it did.

The Measure of Faith

Jesus demonstrated the God-kind of faith to His disciples, and then He told them that they, too, had that kind of faith — the faith that a man believes with his heart, says with his mouth what he believes, and it comes to pass.

Someone might say, "I want that kind of faith. I am going to pray that God will give it to me." However, you don't need to pray for it; you already have it!

"For I say, through the grace given unto me, to every man that is among you, not to think of himself more highly than he ought to think; but to think soberly, according as God hath dealt to every man the measure of faith" (Rom. 12:3).

Notice that Paul wrote this to believers, because he says, "to every man that is among you." The epistle of Romans was not written to the sinners in the world; it is a letter to Christians, because it is addressed "To all that be in Rome, beloved of God, called to be saints . . ." (Rom. 1:7). And in it, Paul tells them that God has given "to every man the measure of faith."

Paul also said, "For by grace are ye saved through faith; and that not of yourselves: it is the gift of God" (Eph. 2:8). Paul is saying here that this faith is not of yourself. He is not referring to grace, because everyone knows that grace is of God.

Paul is saying that the faith by which we are saved is not of ourselves; it is not a natural, human faith. It is given to sinners by God. And how does God give the sinner faith to be saved?

Romans 10:17 says, *"So then faith cometh by hearing, and hearing by the word of God."* In these verses Paul has said faith: (1) is given, (2) is dealt, and (3) comes.

Believing and Saying — The Key to Faith

Notice the words of Romans 10:8, *"But what saith it? The word is nigh thee, even IN THY MOUTH, and IN THY HEART: that is, THE WORD OF FAITH, which we preach."*

How does this compare with the words of Jesus in Mark 11:23? Paul's writings to the Romans agree exactly with what Jesus told His disciples when He said, *"Whosoever shall say . . . and shall not doubt in his heart, but shall believe . . . shall have whatsoever he saith."*

We see here the basic principle inherent in the God-kind of faith: believing with the heart and saying it with the mouth. Jesus believed it, and He said it. God believed it, and He said it, speaking the earth into existence.

Verses 9 and 10 of this same tenth chapter of Romans say, *"That if thou shalt confess with thy mouth the Lord Jesus, and shalt believe in thine heart that God hath raised him from the dead, thou shalt be saved. For with the heart man believeth unto righteousness; and with the mouth confession is made unto salvation."*

A measure of faith is dealt to the sinner through hearing the Word. Then he uses it to create the reality of salvation in his own life.

When Christians are asked, "When were you saved?" they often answer by saying something like, "About 9 o'clock on the night of July 10."

They are mistaken, however. God saved them nearly 2,000 years ago! It only became a reality to them when they believed it and confessed it.

Salvation belongs to everyone. Every man and woman in this world has a legal right to salvation. Jesus died for the whole world, not just for you and me. When the truth is preached to the sinner, it causes faith to come. When he believes and confesses, he creates the reality of it in his own life by his faith.

ROMANS 10:13,14,17
13 For whosoever shall call upon the name of the Lord shall be saved.
14 How then shall they call on him in whom they have not believed? and how shall they believe in him of whom they have not heard? and how shall they hear without a preacher? . . .
17 So then faith cometh by hearing, and hearing by the word of God.

Just as faith comes from hearing the Word of God, so does anything we receive from God. The God-kind of faith comes by hearing God's Word. In other words, God causes the God-kind of faith to come into the hearts of those who hear.

No wonder Jesus said, *"Take heed therefore how ye hear"* (Luke 8:18). You can't let it go in one ear and out the other, because that won't do any good. Faith won't come. If you act as if the Word of God were some fairy tale, faith will not come. But when you accept it reverently and sincerely — when you act upon it — faith comes.

Paul wrote to the Church at Corinth, *"We having the same spirit of faith, according as it is written, I believed, and therefore have I spoken; we also believe, and therefore speak"* (2 Cor. 4:13).

Paul said we have the same spirit of faith. And what belonged to the Church at Corinth belongs to the Church today. On no occasion did Paul or any of the apostles ever write to encourage the people to believe; never did they tell them to have faith.

Our having to encourage believers to believe or have faith is a result of the Word of God's having lost its reality to us. We *are* believers!

When our children are away from home, we don't have to write them and say, "Be sure to keep breathing." They will continue to breathe as long as they are alive. Neither do we have to encourage believers to believe, because that is what they are — believers.

How many of us realize that our words dominate us? *"Thou art snared with the words of thy mouth,"* we read in Proverbs 6:2. Another version says, "Thou art taken captive with the words of thy mouth."

A young man once told me he never was defeated until he confessed that he was. One Baptist minister put it this way: "You said you could not, and the moment you said it, you were

defeated. You said you did not have faith, and doubt rose up like a giant and bound you. You are imprisoned with your own words. You talk failure, and failure holds you in bondage."

Defeat and failure do not belong to the child of God. *God never made a failure!* God made us new creatures. We are not born of the will of the flesh or the will of man, but of the will of God. We are created in Christ Jesus. Failures are man-made. They are made by wrong believing and wrong thinking.

First John 4:4 says, *"greater is he that is in you, than he that is in the world."* Learn to trust the Greater One who is in you. He is mightier than anything in the world.

God created the universe with words! Words filled with faith are the most powerful things in all the world.

The key to the God-kind of faith is *believing* with the heart and *confessing* with the mouth.

Our lips can make us millionaires or keep us paupers.

Our lips can make us victors or keep us captives.

We can fill our words with faith, or we can fill them with doubt.

We can fill our words with love that will melt the coldest heart, or we can fill them with hate and poison.

We can fill our words with love that will help the discouraged and brokenhearted; with faith that will stir heaven.

We can make our words breathe the very atmosphere of heaven.

Our faith will never rise above the

words of our lips. Jesus told the woman with the issue of blood that her faith had made her whole.

Thoughts may come, and they may persist in staying. But if we refuse to put those thoughts into words, they die unborn!

Cultivate the habit of thinking big things. Learn to use words that will react upon your own spirit.

Faith's confessions create realities. Realization follows the confession. Confession precedes possession.

Memory Text:
"But what saith it? The word is nigh thee, even in thy mouth, and in thy heart: that is, the word of faith, which we preach" (Rom. 10:8).

THE LESSON IN ACTION: *"But be ye doers of the word, and not hearers only ..."* (James 1:22).

Lesson 22

Actions That Correspond With Faith

Bible Texts: James 2:14-22; Matthew 7:24-27

Central Truth: The actions of a doer of the Word coincide with his confession.

One of the greatest mistakes believers make is to confess their faith in the Word of God, yet, at the same time, contradict their confession by wrong actions.

We say we are trusting God to provide for our financial needs. But at the same time we worry about how we're going to pay our bills. One minute we confess that the Word of God is true, and the next we repudiate everything we've said by wrong actions. Our actions must correspond with our believing if we are to receive from God.

Faith Made Perfect

JAMES 2:14-22

14 What doth it profit, my brethren, though a man say he hath faith, and have not works? can faith save him?
15 If a brother or sister be naked, and destitute of daily food,
16 And one of you say unto them, Depart in peace, be ye warmed and filled; notwithstanding ye give them not those things which are needful to the body; what doth it profit?
17 Even so faith, if it hath not works, is dead, being alone.
18 Yea, a man may say, Thou hast faith, and I have works: shew me thy faith without thy works, and I will shew thee my faith by my works.
19 Thou believest that there is but one God;

thou doest well: the devils also believe, and tremble.
20 But wilt thou know, O vain man, that faith without works is dead?
21 Was not Abraham our father justified by works, when he had offered Isaac his son upon the altar?
22 Seest thou how faith wrought with his works, and by works was faith made perfect?

Weymouth's translation of verses 14 and 22 reads, "What good is it, my brethren, if a man professes to have faith and yet his actions do not correspond? ...You notice that his faith was co-operating with his actions, and that by his actions his faith was perfected ..."

Some have thought the Book of James was written about salvation and was addressed to the unbeliever. However, James was not writing to the unsaved, but to *believers*. James said, *"What doth it profit, MY BRETHREN..."* James was writing to his brothers and sisters in Christ, pointing out that faith without corresponding actions won't work for them, even though they are believers.

James said, *"But be ye doers of the word, and not hearers only, deceiving your own selves"* (James 1:22). Another translation reads, "...

85

deluding your own selves."

There are many self-deluded people who blame their problems on the devil or some individual when really they have deluded themselves. This is because they are not doers of the Word.

The actions of a doer of the Word coincide with his confession!

The Storms of Life

MATTHEW 7:24-27

24 Therefore whosoever heareth these sayings of mine, and doeth them, I will liken him unto a wise man, which built his house upon a rock:
25 And the rain descended, and the floods came, and the winds blew, and beat upon that house; and it fell not: for it was founded upon a rock.
26 And every one that heareth these sayings of mine, and doeth them not, shall be likened unto a foolish man, which built his house upon the sand:
27 And the rain descended, and the floods came, and the winds blew, and beat upon that house; and it fell: and great was the fall of it.

The storms of life come to us all. They may be storms of sickness, financial difficulty, family problems, or some other test. It isn't the storms of life that defeat us, however. If storms defeated us, they would defeat all of us. No, it's our reaction to the storms that defeats us.

As the winds blow and the floods come, he who is a doer of the Word will hold fast to his confession of faith, because he knows God cannot fail. If sickness comes, he stands his ground and refuses to accept it. Others may

be defeated in the same test.

Those who are not defeated by life's storms act on God's Word. Those who are defeated may be truly saved, yet their actions do not correspond with their faith.

The same wind and storm came upon both houses in our text. The reason one was destroyed and the other wasn't is because the wise man was a doer of the Word, and the foolish man wasn't.

Many profess Christ and declare they believe the Bible from Genesis to Revelation, yet they are not *doers of* the Word. They are *talkers about* the Word. There is a difference.

The "talkers" have mentally assented that the Word of God is true, but it doesn't do them any good, because they are not making it their own. They are not claiming its promises.

Trusting in the Lord Is Trusting in His Word

The way to make God's Word your own is to act upon it. Do what it says. *"Trust in the Lord with all thine heart; and lean not unto thine own understanding"* (Prov. 3:5).

You cannot trust in the Lord without trusting His Word. God and His Word are one, just as you and your word are one. If your word is not good, you are not good. If God's Word isn't any good, He isn't any good. But *His Word is good,* and He watches over His Word!

"Then said the Lord unto me, Thou hast well seen: for I will hasten my

word to perform it" (Jer. 1:12). Another version reads, "... I watch over my word to perform it."

If you don't take the Word to be yours, God doesn't have anything to use to bring good to your life. He wants you to have what His Word promises. But if you don't act upon His Word, then He doesn't have anything to work with to bring good into your life.

When I trust in the Word with all my heart, stop leaning upon human reasoning, and stop looking to people for deliverance, I have actions that correspond with my faith. My actions are in perfect fellowship with my confession of faith.

It has taken some of us a long time to learn this, and it will take others longer, because they have been walking in the wrong pathway. Their minds are so cluttered with human reasoning that it will take a while to renew their minds with the Word of God until their actions correspond with their confession of faith.

Until there are corresponding actions, there will be continual failure in life. I can confess and say that God is the strength of my life, but if I continue to talk about my weaknesses and lack of faith, I will be defeated, because there is no corresponding action.

Resorting to human methods instead of trusting the Lord brings confusion to my spirit. It brings weakness and failure to my life. There is just one thing to do: Turn to God's Word and act upon it.

Our worst enemy is the flesh. The flesh and natural human reasoning limit us to our own abilities. We look to circumstances, problems, tests, and storms, and say we can't. The language of doubt, the flesh, and the senses is, "I can't. I haven't the ability, the opportunity, or the strength. I'm limited." But the language of faith says, "*I can do all things through Christ which strengtheneth me*" (Phil. 4:13).

Paul didn't say he could do all things because he was an apostle and had special power or grace. He said, "*I can do all things through Christ...*" We have this same access to Christ.

Paul said, "*Therefore if any man be in Christ, he is a new creature: old things are passed away; behold, all things are become new*" (2 Cor. 5:17). You are a new creature in Christ, too. Christ doesn't belong to Paul any more than He belongs to you.

The language of faith says, "I can do all things through Christ. Our Father strengthens me. I cannot be conquered, and I cannot be defeated."

If natural forces come against you, they cannot defeat you, because there aren't enough natural forces in all the world to conquer the Holy Spirit dwelling in you. "*... Greater is he that is in you, than he that is in the world*" (1 John 4:4). You are fortified from within!

I have learned how to put the Greater One to work for me. Not only am I born of God and a partaker of His love, but I have dwelling in me the Spirit of the One who raised Jesus from the dead.

I have God's wisdom, strength, and ability in me. I am learning how to let His wisdom govern my intellect. I am allowing Him to govern my mind and speak through my lips. I am daring to think God's thoughts after Him.

I am daring to say in the presence of my enemies, "God is my ability."

"Thou preparest a table before me in the presence of mine enemies ..." (Ps. 23:5). *"... The Lord is the strength of my life; of whom shall I be afraid?"* (Ps. 27:1). God has made me greater than my enemies. God has made me put my heel on the neck of weakness, fear, and inability.

The strength of God is mine. I am not trusting in my own strength, because the Bible doesn't say a word about my being strong. It says that God is my strength.

Many people are struggling and are trying to do something themselves. They get up to testify, and they ask everyone to pray that they will "hold out to the end." But God doesn't want you to hold out like that. He wants you to let Him do it. *Wrap yourself in the promises of God!*

I once heard the story of a man who was walking down a railroad track with a pack on his back. When he came to a section gang repairing the railroad, he thought the foreman was going to order him off the track, so he showed him a ticket. The foreman told him that it didn't give him the right to walk down the track.

Many people are on the right track — but they ought to be riding instead of walking. Also, they should check their baggage, because the Bible says they don't have to carry it: *"Casting all your care upon him; for he careth for you"* (1 Peter 5:7).

Memory Text:
"What doth it profit, my brethren, though a man say he hath faith, and have not works? ..." (James 2:14).

THE LESSON IN ACTION: *"But be ye doers of the word, and not hearers only ..."* (James 1:22).

Lesson 23

How To Write Your Own Ticket With God

Bible Texts: Mark 5:25-34; 1 Samuel 17:45-47,49,50,54; Luke 15:18-20,24

Central Truth: If we find ourselves at the bottom of life's ladder, it is because that is all we have believed for. When we talk and believe right, we will climb to the top.

The four steps to faith outlined in this lesson are so simple, they almost seem foolish. But in Jesus' ministry on earth, He talked in terms that even the uneducated could understand. He talked about vineyards and orchards, sheepfolds and shepherds. He illustrated spiritual truths in such a simple way that the common people could understand them. His message was clear and concise, never complicated.

MARK 5:25-34

25 And a certain woman, which had an issue of blood twelve years,

26 And had suffered many things of many physicians, and had spent all that she had, and was nothing bettered, but rather grew worse,

27 When she had heard of Jesus, came in the press behind, and touched his garment.

28 For she said, If I may touch but his clothes, I shall be whole.

29 And straightway the fountain of her blood was dried up; and she felt in her body that she was healed of that plague.

30 And Jesus, immediately knowing in himself that virtue had gone out of him, turned him about in the press, and said, Who touched my clothes?

31 And his disciples said unto him, Thou seest the multitude thronging thee, and sayest thou, Who touched me?

32 And he looked round about to see her that had done this thing.

33 But the woman fearing and trembling, knowing what was done in her, came and fell down before him, and told him all the truth.

34 And he said unto her, Daughter, thy faith hath made thee whole; go in peace, and be whole of thy plague.

Step 1: Say It

What is the first thing this woman did? Verse 28 says, *"For she said, If I may touch but his clothes, I shall be whole."*

Someone had told this woman about Jesus. She knew He was healing people. Having this information, what was her first step in receiving healing? The first thing she did was to *say it.*

There is God-ward side and a man-ward side to every battle, every victory, and everything else we receive from God. We have our part to play. There is something we must do. God will not fail. If there is any failure, it is on our part. However, if we do our part, we can be sure there will be an answer and a victory.

This woman could have made a negative confession, and that would have been what she received. She could have said there wasn't any use; she had suffered so long and had been to so many doctors. She could have said that perhaps it would be best for her to die.

But she did not speak negatively; she spoke positively. She said, "If I may touch but his clothes, I shall be whole." And it came to pass — because we can have what we say.

Therefore, the first step in writing our own ticket with God is: *Say it.* If we are defeated, we are defeated with our own lips: *"Thou art snared with the words of thy mouth, thou art taken with the words of thy mouth"* (Prov. 6:2).

Step 2: Do It

It wouldn't have done this woman any good whatsoever to have said, "If I may touch but his clothes, I shall be whole" without also acting upon it. Our actions either defeat us or put us over. According to our actions, we either receive or are kept from receiving. The woman with the issue of blood said it and acted upon it. She touched His clothes.

Step 3: Receive It

First, the woman said it. She confessed her faith. Then she acted upon that faith by reaching out and touching the Master. Step three, she received her healing. She felt in her body that she was healed of the plague.

Notice that the feeling and the healing *followed* the saying and the acting. Most people want the feeling and the healing *first;* then they think they will have the saying and the doing. But it doesn't work that way. You have to have the saying and the doing first. *Then* you will have the feeling and the healing.

Jesus perceived that power had gone out of him. The whole world has become concerned about nuclear bombs because they release radioactive material into the atmosphere — power that cannot be seen or felt, but power that is deadly and dangerous. Yet there is an unseen power at work in the earth that is neither deadly nor dangerous. That power is always present everywhere. That power can deliver us from anything that binds or hurts us. It is the power of God.

Step 4: Tell It

Verse 33 tells us that the woman with the issue of blood acknowledged what she had done. She *". . . told him all the truth."* Jesus wants us to tell it so others might receive.

The first step in writing our own ticket is: *Say it.* The fourth step is: *Tell it.* There is a difference. At first the woman said what she *believed.* Then she told what *had happened.*

We have to say some things in faith before we ever receive them from God. People say the wrong thing because they believe the wrong thing. When they start believing and saying the right thing, that is what they will have.

1 SAMUEL 17:45-47,49,50,54

45 Then said David to the Philistine, Thou comest to me with a sword, and with a spear, and with a shield: but I come to thee in the name of the Lord of hosts, the God of the armies of Israel, whom thou hast defied.
46 This day will the Lord deliver thee into mine hand; and I will smite thee, and take thine head from thee; and I will give the carcases of the host of the Philistines this day unto the fowls of the air, and to the wild beasts of the earth; that all the earth may know that there is a God in Israel.
47 And all this assembly shall know that the Lord saveth not with the sword and spear: for the battle is the Lord's, and he will give you into our hands ...
49 And David put his hand in his bag, and took thence a stone, and slang it, and smote the Philistine in his forehead, that the stone sunk into his forehead; and he fell upon his face to the earth.
50 So David prevailed over the Philistine with a sling and with a stone, and smote the Philistine, and slew him ...
54 So David took the head of the Philistine, and brought it to Jerusalem ...

When David slew the giant with his shepherd's sling, he knew he could write his own ticket with God. He knew God would do anything he said. And in the above verses, we see how David used these four steps to write his own ticket with God.

First, he *said it: "This day will the Lord deliver thee into mine hand ..."* (v. 46). David had faith — not in his own strength, but in the strength of his God. David knew that in his own might he was powerless against this Philistine. But he was not trusting in his own might; he was trusting in the Lord.

Then David acted upon his faith: *"And David put his hand in his bag, and took thence a stone, and slang it, and smote the Philistine in his forehead, that the stone sunk into his forehead; and he fell upon his face to the earth"* (v. 49).

If David had been led by his natural senses — if he had listened to human reasoning — he would have known it would be impossible to kill a giant with a shepherd's sling. But he was tuned to the inner voice of faith, not the outer voice of human reasoning, and the victory was his. He received victory for the Israelites over their enemies the Philistines. (This is step three.)

Then David took step four. News of the day's great victory was published throughout the land: *"And David took the head of the Philistine, and brought it to Jerusalem ..."* (v. 54).

Too few people know they can write their own ticket with God. The reason God hasn't done any more for them is because they haven't said more; they haven't acted more. All they have today is the result of what they said yesterday.

If you are at the bottom of the ladder, it is because that is all you have believed for. If you will talk right and believe right, you will climb to the top.

Can a sinner use these four steps to write his own ticket with God? Can the sinner take these four steps to salvation? The following passage proves he can.

LUKE 15:18-20,24

18 I will arise and go to my father, and will say unto him, Father, I have sinned against heaven, and before thee,

19 And am no more worthy to be called thy son: make me as one of thy hired servants.

20 And he arose, and came to his father. But when he was yet a great way off, his father saw him, and had compassion, and ran, and fell on his neck, and kissed him . . .

24 For this my son was dead, and is alive again; he was lost, and is found. And they began to be merry.

In this story Jesus told about the prodigal son, we see that the first thing the son did was to *say it: "I will arise and go to my father, and will say unto him . . ."* (v. 18). He confessed his faith and his need. Then he *acted: "And he arose, and came to his father"* (v. 20). He picked himself up from the squalor of his sinful life and returned home.

When he did so, he *received* full pardon and was restored to his father: *". . . his father saw him, and had compassion, and ran, and fell on his neck, and kissed him"* (v. 20). The rejoicing father was quick to *tell* the good news that his wandering son had come home: *"For this my son was dead, and is alive again; he was lost, and is found . . ."* (v. 24).

If those who are out of fellowship with God the Father will humble themselves as the prodigal son did and will take these four simple steps to salvation, God will run to meet them, and He will bring them into full fellowship with Himself.

Memory Text:

"And he said unto her, Daughter, thy faith hath made thee whole; go in peace, and be whole of thy plague" (Mark 5:34).

THE LESSON IN ACTION: *"But be ye doers of the word, and not hearers only . . ."* (James 1:22).

Lesson 24

Doubt, Thief of God's Greater Blessings

Bible Texts: Matthew 14:22-31; Matthew 17:14-20; Mark 4:35-40

Central Truth: Doubt will rob the believer of God's best for his life.

In today's lesson we will concentrate on some examples of doubt we find in familiar Bible stories.

Faith To Walk on Water

MATTHEW 14:22-31

22 And straightway Jesus constrained his disciples to get into a ship, and to go before him unto the other side, while he sent the multitudes away.

23 And when he had sent the multitudes away, he went up into a mountain apart to pray: and when the evening was come, he was there alone.

24 But the ship was now in the midst of the sea, tossed with waves: for the wind was contrary.

25 And in the fourth watch of the night Jesus went unto them, walking on the sea.

26 And when the disciples saw him walking on the sea, they were troubled, saying, It is a spirit; and they cried out for fear.

27 But straightway Jesus spake unto them, saying, Be of good cheer; it is I; be not afraid.

28 And Peter answered him and said, Lord, if it be thou, bid me come unto thee on the water.

29 And he said, Come. And when Peter was come down out of the ship, he walked on the water, to go to Jesus.

30 But when he saw the wind boisterous, he was afraid; and beginning to sink, he cried, saying, Lord, save me.

31 And immediately Jesus stretched forth his hand, and caught him, and said unto him, O thou of little faith, wherefore didst thou doubt?

In this story, Jesus sent His disciples across the sea while He went alone to a mountain to pray.

In the fourth watch of the night (between 3 and 6 o'clock the next morning), the disciples saw Jesus walking toward them on the water. Thinking they were seeing a ghost, they cried out with fear. Jesus spoke reassuringly, "It is I; be not afraid." Impetuous Peter shouted, "Lord, if it is really You, bid me come to You." Jesus answered with one word: "Come."

Peter started out in faith — and as long as he kept his eyes on Jesus, he did just fine. But when he took his eyes off Jesus and looked at the circumstances surrounding him — the wind whipping the sea about him — he became afraid and began to sink. "Lord, save me!" he cried.

Jesus took Peter's hand and led him back into the boat, rebuking him with the words, "O thou of little faith, wherefore didst thou doubt?"

Faith is acting upon the Word of God. As long as Peter acted on Jesus' word to him, he was all right. But when he began to doubt — when he became afraid and quit acting on the words of Jesus — he began to sink.

Jesus didn't intend for Peter to sink. He meant for Peter to walk back to the ship with Him. Doubt robbed Peter of this blessing.

Doubt and fear go hand in hand, but faith and love also go hand in hand: "... *perfect love casteth out fear* ..." (1 John 4:18).

Faith To Cast Out Devils

MATTHEW 17:14-20
14 And when they were come to the multitude, there came to him a certain man, kneeling down to him, and saying,
15 Lord, have mercy on my son: for he is lunatick, and sore vexed: for ofttimes he falleth into the fire, and oft into the water.
16 And I brought him to thy disciples, and they could not cure him.
17 Then Jesus answered and said, O faithless and perverse generation, how long shall I be with you? how long shall I suffer you? bring him hither to me.
18 And Jesus rebuked the devil; and he departed out of him: and the child was cured from that very hour.
19 Then came the disciples to Jesus apart, and said, Why could not we cast him out?
20 And Jesus said unto them, Because of your unbelief: for verily I say unto you, If ye have faith as a grain of mustard seed, ye shall say unto this mountain, Remove hence to yonder place; and it shall remove; and nothing shall be impossible unto you.

In the above passage, what was Jesus' explanation for the disciples' failure to heal the demon-possessed boy? It was because of their doubt or unbelief (v. 20). But did the disciples actually have the power to cast the demon out? Yes, according to Matthew 10:1, "*And when he had called unto him his twelve disciples, he gave them power against unclean spirits, to cast them out, and to heal all manner of sickness and all manner of disease.*"

We often hear Christians say they need more power to do more for God. However, that is not their trouble at all! If they have the Holy Spirit, they have the power. They think if they had more power, it would work automatically — but it works by faith. *The problem is a lack of faith, not a lack of power!*

It is doubt that is robbing people of God's best. Jesus didn't tell the disciples that their failure to cast the devil out was because they didn't have the power; He said it was because of their unbelief.

How much faith does it take to cast out demons? Jesus said in the above Scripture passage that faith no larger than a grain of mustard seed could move an entire mountain.

Every Spirit-filled believer has within him enough power to claim God's very best for his life! If he is living beneath his privileges, it is not because of a lack of power, but because of a failure to release that power through faith.

Faith To Still a Storm

MARK 4:35-40
35 And the same day, when the even was come, he saith unto them, Let us pass over unto the other side.
36 And when they had sent away the multitude, they took him even as he was in

the ship. And there were also with him other little ships.

37 And there arose a great storm of wind, and the waves beat into the ship, so that it was now full.

38 And he was in the hinder part of the ship, asleep on a pillow: and they awake him, and say unto him, Master, carest thou not that we perish?

39 And he arose, and rebuked the wind, and said unto the sea, Peace, be still. And the wind ceased, and there was a great calm.

40 And he said unto them, Why are ye so fearful? how is it that ye have no faith?

One evening, after a full day of preaching to the multitudes, Jesus told His disciples, who were gathered about Him in a boat, "Let us pass over unto the other side." He was weary and promptly fell into a deep sleep in the back of the boat, oblivious to the storm that arose. He continued to sleep peacefully despite the waves that pounded the little boat. His disciples were anything but peaceful. As the howling winds grew and the boat filled with water, the disciples awakened Jesus, saying, "Don't You even care that our boat is about to sink and we'll all die?" They had forgotten Jesus' words as they had started out on their journey.

Jesus stood up, rebuked the wind, and stilled the storm. The Sea of Galilee became calm and peaceful once more. Then He turned to His disciples and rebuked them: "Why did you doubt Me? Why are you so full of fear? Where is your faith? Didn't I tell you at the outset of this journey that we would cross to the other side? Why didn't you believe Me?"

The disciples had allowed doubt and fear to come into their hearts, driving out faith in Jesus' promise that they would make it safely to the other side. Once again the thief named Doubt had triumphed.

Let us notice the similarities in these three Biblical illustrations. In each one, Jesus rebuked the disciples for their unbelief (Matt. 14:31; Matt. 17:20; Mark 4:40), and in each one He solved the problem the disciples, through their lack of faith, had failed to solve.

In all three instances, the disciples possessed the power to handle the circumstances.

In each instance, the thief of doubt kept the disciples from receiving God's best for them. His highest and best was for them to receive by their faith.

If we, too, will only utilize the power that is within us and act on God's Word, we will achieve the blessings God has planned for our lives.

Memory Text:
"For verily I say unto you, That whosoever shall say unto this mountain, Be thou removed, and be thou cast into the sea; and shall not doubt in his heart, but shall believe that those things which he saith shall come to pass; he shall have whatsoever he saith" (Mark 11:23).

THE LESSON IN ACTION: *"But be ye doers of the word, and not hearers only . . ."* (James 1:22).

You Can Have What You Say

Bible Texts: Mark 11:23; Numbers 13:17,18,25,27,28,30-32; Numbers 14:6-9

Central Truth: It was not the giants in the land of Canaan who kept the Israelites out, but the giants of fear in their hearts.

Our text for this lesson, Mark 11:23, is one I frequently use in teaching on faith, because in it we see the "faith formula" for moving whatever mountains may be present in our lives.

Whether your particular mountain is sickness, unsaved loved ones, financial difficulties, or family problems, you can find the solution in this verse of Scripture.

MARK 11:23
23 For verily I say unto you, That whosoever shall say unto this mountain, Be thou removed, and be thou cast into the sea; and shall not doubt in his heart, but shall believe that those things which he saith shall come to pass; he shall have whatsoever he saith.

The last phrase says, *"he shall have whatsoever he SAITH."* In other words, you can have whatever you *say* you can have. *What you SAY is your faith speaking.* This works in a negative way just as it works in a positive way, as we see in the Old Testament story of the 12 spies who were sent into Canaan to spy out the land.

A Report of Fear

NUMBERS 13:17,18,25,27,28,30-32
17 And Moses sent them to spy out the land of Canaan, and said unto them, Get you up this way southward, and go up into the mountain:
18 And see the land, what it is; and the people that dwelleth therein, whether they be strong or weak, few or many...
25 And they returned from searching of the land after forty days. . . .
27 And they told him, and said, We came unto the land whither thou sentest us, and surely it floweth with milk and honey; and this is the fruit of it.
28 Nevertheless the people be strong that dwell in the land, and the cities are walled, and very great: and moreover we saw the children of Anak there. . . .
30 And Caleb stilled the people before Moses, and said, Let us go up at once, and possess it; for we are well able to overcome it.
31 But the men that went up with him said, We be not able to go up against the people; for they are stronger than we.
32 And they brought up an evil report of the land which they had searched unto the children of Israel, saying, The land, through which we have gone to search it, is a land that eateth up the inhabitants thereof; and all the people that we saw in it are men of a great stature.

Of the 12 spies who went into Canaan to search out the land, only two, Caleb and Joshua, were men of faith and vision. They said, *"Let us go up at once, and possess it; for we are well able to overcome it."*

The other 10 came back with a negative, fearful report of giants in the land. The Bible calls their report "an evil report." Why? It was a report of doubt and fear. What, then, is a *good* report? A report of faith.

The 10 fearful spies were in the majority, and the children of Israel accepted the majority report. When they did, they were saying they couldn't take the land. And they got exactly what they *said.*

These spies and the rest of that generation of Israelites — with the exception of Joshua and Caleb — never saw the Promised Land. They believed that they couldn't take it, and they didn't. They wandered in the wilderness until they died. What they *said* came to pass!

Theirs is an example of faith in reverse. After all, *even when you doubt, you are believing something!* You are believing in defeat. You are believing the wrong thing.

You always get in your life what you believe for and what you say. If you don't believe what you are saying, you shouldn't say it, because if you keep saying something long enough, those words eventually will register on your spirit. And once they are registered on your spirit, they will control your life.

A Report of Faith

NUMBERS 14:6-9

6 And Joshua the son of Nun, and Caleb the son of Jephunneh, which were of them that searched the land, rent their clothes:

7 And they spake unto all the company of the children of Israel, saying, The land, which we passed through to search it, is an exceeding good land.

8 If the Lord delight in us, then he will bring us into this land, and give it us; a land which floweth with milk and honey.

9 Only rebel not ye against the Lord, neither fear ye the people of the land; for they are bread for us: their defence is departed from them, and the Lord is with us: fear them not.

Notice the good report of Joshua and Caleb. Their trust was in the Lord, and their hearts were filled with faith that God was able to bring them into the land He had promised to their forefathers. Twice in verse nine they admonished the people not to fear. And what was the result of their report of faith? They were the only two men of their generation to enter the Promised Land! You can have what you say.

Many people ask me why they can't get healed. I always smile and tell them they already have said they can't. Their words give them away. You can locate people by what they say.

Before praying for people, I usually try to get them to make some kind of a confession of their faith. I ask them if they will be healed when I lay hands on them and pray. If they answer that they *hope* they will, I tell them they won't because they are in *hope*, not *faith.*

Others make a confession with some hesitancy, and that hesitancy is what defeats them. (It is "the little foxes that spoil the vine.") Those who have a quick confession full of faith receive almost instantly.

It is not something big that keeps God's children from being healed. It wasn't the giants of the land of Canaan who kept the children of Israel out. It wasn't the giants who defeated them. If it had been the giants, they would have defeated Joshua and Caleb also. No, the people defeated themselves by their own wrong thinking and their own declaration of unbelief.

So it is not the giants in life who defeat you. It is not the storms of life that defeat you. *If you are defeated, it is because you have defeated yourself.* You have defeated yourself by wrong thinking, wrong believing, and wrong speaking. You can have what you say.

Caleb and Joshua said they were able to overcome the giants. After 40 years of wandering in the wilderness, and after all the people of that generation who had accepted the evil report of the 10 spies had died, Joshua became the people's leader. He and Caleb led them to victory.

When Caleb came to Joshua and said, "Give me this mountain," Joshua looked back over the years and realized that their talking right had won them victory before. Wanting to locate Caleb, he asked him if he were able to take the mountain. (Joshua wanted to hear Caleb's confession of faith.) He told Caleb that there were giants in the mountain. But Caleb, full of faith, said that he was well able to take it — and he did take it.

Many things happen because we expect them to happen a certain way. They happen because we believe and talk it until it comes to pass. I have found this true in my own experience.

Some time ago I read that when one gets older, the arteries in his brain aren't as soft as they were when he was younger; they gradually keep hardening.

I had reached the place where I couldn't remember things as well as I once did. I went along this way for a while until I realized there wasn't any need for it. The mind is part of my inward being and spirit, and it never grows old. The very moment I started believing right and talking right, I could quote all the Scripture I had ever known, and my memory actually improved.

We fail sometimes because we get ready to fail. We prepare to fail. We think it, believe it, and then do it. As believers, however, we have no business talking failure or doubt. We should talk faith.

Memory Text:
"For verily I say unto you, That whosoever shall say unto this mountain, Be thou removed, and be thou cast into the sea; and shall not doubt in his heart, but shall believe that those things which he saith shall come to pass; he shall have whatsoever he saith" (Mark 11:23).

THE LESSON IN ACTION: *"But be ye doers of the word, and not hearers only ..."* (James 1:22).

Lesson 26

How To Train the Human Spirit

Bible Texts: Joshua 1:8; James 1:22; Proverbs 4:20-22

Central Truth: God will use our own spirit to guide us.

Just as the human mind can be trained intellectually, so the human spirit can be trained spiritually. It can be built up in strength just as the body can be built up.

In this lesson we will look at four ways this can be accomplished:

1. Meditating in the Word of God.
2. Practicing the Word of God.
3. Giving the Word of God first place.
4. Instantly obeying the voice of our spirit.

As we apply these four principles to our daily lives, we can come to know the will of God even in the minor details of life.

God communicates with our spirit, not with our reasoning faculties. As we instantly obey our spirit, we will find we are obeying the Holy Spirit. God said in His Word, *"The spirit of man is the candle of the Lord, searching all the inward parts of the belly"* (Prov. 20:27). This means that God is going to use our own spirit to guide us. The spirit of man is the candle of the Lord.

Rule 1: Meditating in the Word of God

JOSHUA 1:8

8 This book of the law shall not depart out of thy mouth; but thou shalt meditate therein day and night, that thou mayest observe to do according to all that is written therein: for then thou shalt make thy way prosperous, and then thou shalt have good success.

When God anointed Joshua to lead the children of Israel after Moses' death, God told him at the outset the importance of meditating in the Word. Another translation of the last phrase of Joshua 1:8 says, "You will be able to deal wisely in the things of life." Certainly we wouldn't have good success if we could not deal wisely in the things of life. God told Joshua if he would meditate in the Word, God would make his way prosperous and he would have good success.

The most deeply spiritual men and women I have known are those who give time to meditation. One cannot develop spiritual wisdom without meditation in God's Word.

One pastor once told me he had been trying to make a success of his church. He flew all over the country, visiting many of the larger churches, studying their methods, and trying to find out what made them successful. He brought their programs and ideas back to his church, but they didn't seem to work.

After hearing me teach about meditating in God's Word, he decided to try it. Rather than asking God for things, he set aside a certain time daily for meditating in the Word.

After 30 days had passed, at the close of his Sunday morning sermon, a landslide of souls was at the altar. More people were saved in that one service than had been saved in that church in the previous two years. The people were revived, and the pastor began to have good success.

His testimony can be that of any believer who will follow his example and spend time meditating in God's Word. Shut the world out. If you have ambitions to do something worthwhile, I suggest you begin by taking 10 or 15 minutes daily for meditation. Begin the development of your spirit.

Rule 2: Practicing the Word of God

JAMES 1:22
22 But be ye doers of the word, and not hearers only, deceiving your own selves.

Practicing the Word is what James called being "a doer of the Word." Some people think that being a doer of the Word is keeping the Ten Commandments. Under the New Covenant, however, we have one commandment: the commandment of love.

If you love someone, you won't steal from him. You won't lie about him. Paul said that love is the fulfilling of the law. If you walk in love, you won't break any law that was given to curb sin.

In this verse of Scripture, James is urging believers to do primarily what is written in the epistles: to act upon this Word.

For example, Paul wrote to the Philippians, *"Be careful for nothing; but in every thing by prayer and supplication with thanksgiving let your requests be made known unto God"* (Phil. 4:6).

The Amplified Bible says, "Do not fret or have any anxiety about anything, but in every circumstance and in everything by prayer and petition [definite requests] with thanksgiving continue to make your wants known to God."

Usually we practice only part of this. We don't mind practicing the part that tells us to pray, but if we practice one part and not the other, we are not practicing the Word. We are not a doer of the Word.

First, the Lord said not to fret. If we're going to fret and have anxieties, it isn't going to do any good to make requests. If God said not to fret, this means we can keep from it. God is a just God, and He won't ask us to do something we can't do.

There was a time when I believed that I could make my requests known to God, but I had difficulty believing that I needn't fret.

God, however, said we don't have to fret. So I say, "I refuse to fret or have any anxiety about anything." I take my requests to Him, and then I thank Him. This quiets and pacifies the troubled spirit that the devil would try to make me have. If inner turmoil persists, I simply go right back to this verse and read it again. I keep claiming it.

If we follow Paul's advice and "do not fret or have anxiety about anything," we can believe God for the promise of the verse that follows: *"And the peace of God, which passeth all understanding, shall keep your hearts and minds through Christ Jesus"* (Phil. 4:7).

Many people want what this seventh verse talks about, but they don't want to do what the sixth verse says to do to get it. However, to receive this *"peace . . . which passeth all understanding,"* we must *"Be careful for nothing; but in every thing by prayer and supplication with thanksgiving let your requests be made known unto God"* (v. 6).

"God's peace . . . shall garrison and mount guard" is *The Amplified Bible's* translation of verse seven. It will keep guard over your heart and your spirit.

The education of our spirits comes by practicing the Word. Can you reap the results and have peace without being a doer of the Word? No, you really can't. Be a doer of the Word, and you'll grow spiritually.

Rule 3: Giving the Word First Place

PROVERBS 4:20-22

20 My son, attend to my words; incline thine ear unto my sayings.
21 Let them not depart from thine eyes; keep them in the midst of thine heart.
22 For they are life unto those that find them, and health to all their flesh.

With so many different voices surrounding us, it is difficult to stop and listen to the voice of the Word of God.

Family and friends always are ready to give us their opinions and advice. However, an essential part of training the spiritual man is learning to listen to what God's Word has to say to us. It is giving the Word first place in our lives.

In the verses quoted above, God tells us to do three things with His Word: (1) listen to it; (2) read it; and (3) memorize it. In verse 20 we read, *"incline thine ear unto my sayings."*

Anytime the Bible is being read aloud — in church, in family devotions, on a Gospel radio or television program — give careful attention to its words.

Verse 21 tells us, *"Let them not depart from thine eyes."* In other words, spend time alone reading God's Word. Let it sink deep into your thoughts and your heart. Memorize it, as verse 21 tells us: *"Keep them in the midst of thine heart."*

If we do these three things, we will find that God's Words are *"life unto those that find them, and health to all their flesh"* (v. 22). We will enter into the abundant life in Christ Jesus. We will find physical healing for our bodies. All we need to do is give God's Word first place in our lives.

Rule 4: Instantly Obeying the Voice of Our Spirit

The human spirit has a voice. We call that voice conscience. Sometimes we call it intuition, or we call it an inner voice of guidance. It is our spirit talking to us.

Every man's spirit has a voice,

whether he is saved or unsaved. But the New Birth is a rebirth of the human spirit. Your spirit gets its information as you meditate upon the Word. Learn to obey your spirit.

Your spirit has the life and nature of God in it, because the Holy Spirit dwells within you. The devil can't be giving you the information, because he is not in you; he is on the outside of you.

God has to communicate with you through your spirit, because that is where He is. He isn't in your head. He isn't in your reasoning faculties. He is in your spirit. Your spirit gets its information through Him. Learn to obey your spirit.

Some people say that conscience is not a safe guide, but this isn't always true. The conscience is a safe guide in the Spirit-filled believer because God is dwelling within that believer. The believer's conscience, the voice of his spirit, becomes the voice of God. God is speaking to him. Paul said he obeyed his conscience (Acts 23:1).

"The spirit of man is the candle of the Lord . . ." (Prov. 20:27). God will use your spirit to guide you. He will use it to enlighten you. As your spirit meditates and feeds upon the Word, it becomes a safer guide. It is trained in the Word.

The Holy Spirit does speak a little differently to those of us who have certain ministry gifts. As a rule in the lives of believers, the inward voice is the voice of the human spirit speaking; not the Holy Spirit.

The Holy Spirit often speaks to me about others, but I never hear Him for my own benefit. Why? Because a prophet's ministry isn't given for his benefit; it's given for the benefit of others. I have to receive guidance for myself just as does any other believer: through the inward voice.

As we learn to obey the voice of our spirit, we will come to the place where we know what we should do in all phases of life. The Lord will guide us. *"In all thy ways acknowledge him, and he shall direct thy paths"* (Prov. 3:6).

Memory Text:
"The spirit of man is the candle of the Lord, searching all the inward parts of the belly" (Prov. 20:27).

THE LESSON IN ACTION: *"But be ye doers of the word, and not hearers only . . ."* (James 1:22).

102